Enhancing Undergraduate Learning with
INFORMATION TECHNOLOGY
A WORKSHOP SUMMARY

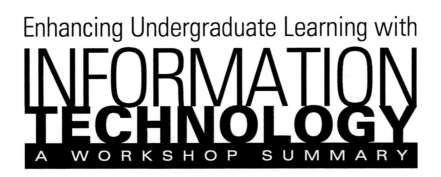

Margaret Hilton, Editor

Center for Education
Division of Behavioral and Social Sciences and Education
National Research Council

NATIONAL ACADEMY PRESS
Washington, DC

NATIONAL ACADEMY PRESS   2101 Constitution Avenue, NW   Washington, DC 20418

NOTICE: The project that is the subject of this report was approved by the Governing Board of the National Research Council, whose members are drawn from the councils of the National Academy of Sciences, the National Academy of Engineering, and the Institute of Medicine. The members of the committee responsible for the report were chosen for their special competences and with regard for appropriate balance.

This study was supported by Grant # ESI-0002231 between the National Academy of Sciences and the National Science Foundation. Any opinions, findings, conclusions, or recommendations expressed in this publication are those of the author(s) and do not necessarily reflect the views of the organizations or agencies that provided support for the project.

THE NATIONAL ACADEMIES

National Academy of Sciences
National Academy of Engineering
Institute of Medicine
National Research Council

The **National Academy of Sciences** is a private, nonprofit, self-perpetuating society of distinguished scholars engaged in scientific and engineering research, dedicated to the furtherance of science and technology and to their use for the general welfare. Upon the authority of the charter granted to it by the Congress in 1863, the Academy has a mandate that requires it to advise the federal government on scientific and technical matters. Dr. Bruce M. Alberts is president of the National Academy of Sciences.

The **National Academy of Engineering** was established in 1964, under the charter of the National Academy of Sciences, as a parallel organization of outstanding engineers. It is autonomous in its administration and in the selection of its members, sharing with the National Academy of Sciences the responsibility for advising the federal government. The National Academy of Engineering also sponsors engineering programs aimed at meeting national needs, encourages education and research, and recognizes the superior achievements of engineers. Dr. Wm. A. Wulf is president of the National Academy of Engineering.

The **Institute of Medicine** was established in 1970 by the National Academy of Sciences to secure the services of eminent members of appropriate professions in the examination of policy matters pertaining to the health of the public. The Institute acts under the responsibility given to the National Academy of Sciences by its congressional charter to be an adviser to the federal government and, upon its own initiative, to identify issues of medical care, research, and education. Dr. Kenneth I. Shine is president of the Institute of Medicine.

The **National Research Council** was organized by the National Academy of Sciences in 1916 to associate the broad community of science and technology with the Academy's purposes of furthering knowledge and advising the federal government. Functioning in accordance with general policies determined by the Academy, the Council has become the principal operating agency of both the National Academy of Sciences and the National Academy of Engineering in providing services to the government, the public, and the scientific and engineering communities. The Council is administered jointly by both Academies and the Institute of Medicine. Dr. Bruce M. Alberts and Dr. Wm. A. Wulf are chairman and vice chairman, respectively, of the National Research Council.

PLANNING GROUP FOR THE WORKSHOP ON THE ROLES OF INFORMATION TECHNOLOGY IN IMPROVING TEACHING AND LEARNING IN UNDERGRADUATE SCIENCE, MATHEMATICS, ENGINEERING, AND TECHNOLOGY EDUCATION

Marshall S. Smith, *Chair*, Education Program Officer, William and Flora Hewlett Foundation

Martha Darling, Educational Consultant, Ann Arbor, Michigan

Deborah Hughes Hallett, Professor of Mathematics, University of Arizona

Jack Wilson, Professor of Management, University of Massachusetts, Amherst, and CEO of UMassOnLine*

NATIONAL RESEARCH COUNCIL STAFF

Jay Labov, Associate Director, Center for Education

Kevin Aylesworth, Senior Program Officer, Center for Education

Margaret Hilton, Program Officer, Center for Education

Terry K. Holmer, Senior Project Assistant, Center for Education

---

*At the time of the workshop, Wilson was Professor of Physics, Information Technology, Engineering, and Management Rensselaer Polytechnic Institute.

Reviewers

This report has been reviewed in draft form by individuals chosen for their diverse perspectives and technical expertise, in accordance with procedures approved by the National Research Council's Report Review Committee. The purpose of this independent review is to provide candid and critical comments that will assist the institution in making the published report as sound as possible and to ensure that the report meets institutional standards for objectivity, evidence, and responsiveness to the study charge. The review comments and draft manuscript remain confidential to protect the integrity of the deliberative process. We wish to thank the following individuals for their participation in the review of this report:

Lara K. Couturier, Brown University
Martha Darling, Consultant, Ann Arbor, MI

Alan Lesgold, University of Pittsburgh
Evelyn T. Patterson, U.S. Air Force Academy
Barbara Sawrey, University of California, San Diego

Although the reviewers listed above have provided many constructive comments and suggestions, they were not asked to endorse the conclusions or recommendations nor did they see the final draft of the report before its release. The review of this report was overseen by Nicholas J. Turro, Columbia University. Appointed by the National Research Council, he was responsible for making certain that an independent examination of this report was carried out in accordance with institutional procedures and that all review comments were carefully considered. Responsibility for the final content of this report rests entirely with the authoring committee and the institution.

Preface

Information Technology (IT) enables exciting new approaches to undergraduate science, mathematics, engineering, and technology (SME&T) education. Cognitive research has begun to illuminate how students learn (National Research Council [NRC], 1999a) providing a basis for design of more effective learning environments and teaching practices (NRC, 1999b). At the same time, personal computers with Internet access, as well as other IT tools, are becoming ubiquitous on many college and university campuses (Web-Based Education Commission, 2000). Encouraged by these developments, small but growing numbers of faculty are transforming traditional SME&T lectures and laboratories into more active learning environments that hold the promise of enhancing undergraduate learning.

Scientists, policy makers, and researchers discussed these developments at a workshop, held at the National Academy of Sciences in June 2000. Presenters described innovative undergraduate courses in a range of SME&T disciplines. Using IT, these courses have been transformed in ways that appear to enhance learning for a diverse spectrum of undergraduate students. However, workshop participants noted that the full educational potential of IT has not yet been realized. Several factors, including the difficulty of assessing student learning in technology-rich environments, the state of current technology, and cultural and institutional factors could pose barriers to rapid deployment of technology in SME&T classrooms.

The breathtaking pace of change in IT makes it virtually impossible to accurately predict its future impact on teaching and learning in undergraduate SME&T education. Nevertheless, many workshop participants felt that it was not only possible, but also essential, to begin planning for what the future might hold. Some presenters identified steps that could be taken to speed development of the educational potential of

IT and support a promising future for SME&T education.

This workshop evolved from a planning process begun in early 2000, when the National Academies created a new Center for Education (CFE). The new Center includes the Academies' Center for Science, Mathematics, and Engineering Education (CSMEE), Board on Testing and Assessment, and Board on International Comparative Studies in Education. To define directions and priorities for future studies, CFE established a Strategic Planning Advisory Group. This advisory group gave high priority to the Center's undertaking studies of the impact of IT in education. As the first step toward such studies, the CFE convened a planning group to develop a workshop on the role of IT in undergraduate SME&T education.

The goal of the workshop was to inform the Strategic Planning Advisory Group, workshop participants, and the public about some issues surrounding the use of IT in education. To reach this goal, the planning group invited workshop presenters to pay particular attention to the following issues:

• What educational technologies currently exist, and how they are being used to transform undergraduate SME&T education;

• What is known about the potential future impact of information technology on teaching and learning at the undergraduate level;

• How to evaluate the impact of IT on teaching and learning; and

• What the future might hold.

The planning group identified topics and speakers for the workshop, and developed the agenda, but did not participate in writing this summary. Both the agenda and this summary build on earlier research into the role of IT in pedagogy and learning, produced by CSMEE's Committee on Information Technology. That committee analyzed and synthesized research about the ability of IT to enable new educational approaches, and identified many examples of such approaches. This synthesis of earlier research was sent to all workshop participants as background reading, providing a broader context for the presentations at the workshop, which focused on a few selected case studies. It is included in this workshop summary as Appendix A.

Contents

1

Innovations in Pedagogy and Technology

I hear and I forget; I see and I remember; I do
and I understand.
—ancient Chinese Proverb

THE ROLE OF TECHNOLOGY

Marshall Smith, chair of the workshop
planning group (and an officer of the William and Flora Hewlett Foundation), opened
the workshop by inviting participants "to
look deeply at the issues of improving teaching and learning." Smith's emphasis on
pedagogy was reflected in the workshop
presentations and discussions. Although
workshop participants believed that information technology (IT) has great potential
to *support* improved science, mathematics,
engineering, and technology (SME&T)
education, most agreed that there was noth-
ing inherent in new technologies, by themselves, that would *determine* improvement.
The participants noted that when IT is used
for administrative purposes (for example, an

instructor posts the course syllabus on the
Internet), it is unlikely to help students
understand and master scientific and technical subjects. Presenters and discussants
focused instead on using IT to enable innovations in pedagogy that can increase learning. Although such innovations are possible without technology, the capabilities of
IT make them easier and more practical.
The new approaches to teaching and learning discussed at the workshop reflect developments in SME&T education, cognitive
science, and educational research.

Traditionally, SME&T courses at U.S.
colleges and universities have been com-
prised of lectures and laboratory sessions.
However, a growing body of research indicates that this traditional approach is not
effective for all undergraduates. Cognitive
scientists have found that students have
different ways of learning and benefit from
different educational approaches (National
Research Council [NRC], 1999a). In 1984,

Godleski argued that lectures best serve students who are intuitive rather than sensory learners, and a decade later, McDermott, Shaffer, and Somers (1994) found that standard physics lectures do not help most students grasp fundamental concepts. Researchers have also found that when SME&T instructors recognize that student learning strategies vary and modify instruction accordingly, more students are able to learn and master these complex disciplines (Felder, 1993, 1996; Tobias, 1992).

Laboratory sessions, too, do not help all students develop a deep understanding of SME&T concepts. Students can perform the experiments carefully, achieve the predetermined outcome, answer questions, and complete the lab report, yet still leave with very little understanding of the concepts they were supposed to learn (Poole and Kidder, 1996). Even in some SME&T courses based on newer curricula, laboratory experiences may emphasize verifying established knowledge and may not correlate with material presented in subsequent lectures (Hilosky, Sutman, and Schmuckler, 1998).

Data on course completion also indicate that many students cannot master SME&T subjects as they are currently taught (Seymour and Hewitt, 1997). Among U.S. students who declared science and engineering majors as freshmen in 1989/1990, fewer than half had completed such a degree 5 years later, and about 22 percent had dropped out altogether (National Science Foundation [NSF], 2000). Among non-

Asian minority students who planned to major in SME&T disciplines as freshmen in 1989/1990, only 25 percent had completed a science or engineering degree after 5 years (NSF, 2000).

In response to these problems, some SME&T educators are experimenting with innovative pedagogical methods. Often, these new approaches are based on research into human cognition, which has identified four elements that are key to enhancing learning (NRC, 1999b, pp. 19-22):

1. Schools and classrooms must be learner centered.

2. Attention must be given to what is taught (information, subject matter), why it is taught (understanding), and what competence or mastery looks like.

3. Formative assessments—ongoing assessments designed to make students' thinking visible to both teachers and students—are essential.

4. Learning is influenced in fundamental ways by the context in which it takes place. A community-centered approach requires that students, teachers, and others share norms that value learning and high standards.

Workshop participants identified several key elements of this new pedagogy. First, instructors who use technology to implement these new approaches to teaching and learning typically move from lecturing, as a "sage on the stage," to becoming a "guide on the side." Although the instructor still plays a critically important role, deciding how and when to intervene to enable and support learning, the focus of the educational process shifts from the instructor towards the learner. Second, in the new paradigm, education can become less abstract, as both students and faculty can create projects or perform research that is useful to employers, community groups, or others outside the classroom. Third, competition to succeed as an individual student or professor at the expense of others is reduced, and collaboration becomes an increasingly powerful learning tool.

Harvard University professor Christopher Dede emphasized the importance of this new approach to pedagogy in his presentation on the educational potential of multiple interactive media. Dede noted that, until recently, many educators viewed IT primarily as a way to increase student access and provide economies of scale for traditional modes of education.[1] However, according to Dede, there is a "new rationale" for using IT in higher education, beyond simply increasing access. Now, more college and university faculty recognize that IT has the power to transform education by supporting shared creation, collaboration, and mastery of knowledge (Dede, 2000; see

also Hanna et al., 2000). Like the growing numbers of scientists who collaborate simultaneously with local and distant colleagues in virtual "knowledge networks," students can use IT to collaborate and to learn.

Information Technology can allow teaching and learning to be transformed in these ways, even when students do not interact with each other face-to-face, according to Dede. He noted that some students who are silent and passive in face-to-face settings "find their voice" and become active participants in technology-mediated communication. Using both synchronous and asynchronous media is important in producing this effect across the full range of learners. However, Dede argued that effective design of learning environments will include careful attention to the role of faculty mentors, as well as to technology. Summarizing his belief that IT is powerful "only if the medium is used well," Dede stated "in the pedagogy lies the power."

To illustrate the importance of using IT to support this new pedagogy, rather than to simply expand delivery of current educational approaches, Ben Shneiderman of the University of Maryland (UMD) suggested using new words. He proposed replacing "Information" in "Information Technology" with "Communication," reflecting the power of IT to support collaborative learning. Several recent comparative studies support Shneiderman's suggestion that IT be used to enhance communication and collaboration among SME&T students. One recent study (Johnson, Johnson, and Smith, 1998) found that cooperative learn-

---

[1]This point was reinforced during the workshop by Professor Richard Larson of MIT. Larson described the growth of private, Web-based education providers, and of partnerships between colleges and universities and these private vendors. Larson said that students anywhere around the world can now access upper-level MIT mathematics course materials at any time of the day or night.

ing promotes higher individual achievement than either competitive or individualistic approaches to learning. Springer, Stanne, and Donovan (1997) analyzed comparative studies of small-group and individual education, concluding that collaborative groups promoted "greater academic achievement, more favorable attitudes toward learning, and increased persistence through SME&T courses and programs." Another meta-analysis (Johnson et al., 1998) reached similar conclusions. Studies of students in biology (Watson and Marshall, 1995), chemistry (Wright, 1996), earth science (Macdonald and Korinek, 1995), and physics (Hake, 1998) all indicated that students collaborating in small groups learned more than those working independently.

Shneiderman also suggested replacing the "Technology" in IT with "Philosophy," in keeping with his view that teachers need a guiding philosophy in order to meet the many goals of undergraduate education (Shneiderman, 1998b). Thus, rather than a technology to transmit information, IT becomes a "philosophy" or pedagogy to enhance human communication and learning.

Taken together, the views of those attending the workshop suggest that IT may make it possible to transform undergraduate SME&T education along the lines shown in Table 1-1.

This new pedagogy reflects current thinking (although not yet current practice) in SME&T education. It is similar to the new educational approaches in primary and secondary schools called for in national standards for science (NRC, 1996), mathematics (National Council of Teachers of Mathematics, 2000), and technology (International Technology Education Association, 2000) education.

When discussing current technological tools for education, presenters and partici-

TABLE 1-1 *How IT Might Transform Undergraduate SME&T Education*

Traditional SME&T Paradigm	New Pedagogical Paradigm
Teacher centered	Learner centered
Instructor delivers information (information may be transmitted via IT)	Students and faculty engage in active learning/problem-solving together
Individualistic (students work on their own, faculty work as individuals within a single discipline)	Collaborative (students work in groups; faculty collaborate with other faculty within and across disciplines)
Abstract	Practical
Academia is an "ivory tower," remote from the outside world	Students create service projects, useful to businesses, the university, or the community
Information Technology transmits information	Information Technology enables communication and learning

pants expressed varying views about their permanence and usefulness. Some agreed with Andries van Dam's assertion that today's Web-based educational offerings are "strictly transitional," while others argued that in some current applications, IT is indeed effectively enhancing SME&T education. However, these disagreements were quickly put aside when participants recalled their focus on innovations in pedagogy, rather than in technology. Rensselaer Polytechnic Institute professor Jack Wilson, who was a member of the earlier Committee on Information Technology, emphasized the importance of saying "loud and clear" that it is time "to focus on the learner and to build our education systems based on the best research."

Whatever their views on current educational technologies for undergraduate learning, participants agreed that such technologies were likely to be very different, and possibly much better in the future. They noted that, based on the predictions and previous application of Moore's Law,[2] IT promises to continue its rapid evolution.

---

[2]According to the Webopedia (www.webopedia. com [10/2/01]): "The observation made in 1965 by Gordon Moore, co-founder of Intel, that the number of transistors per square inch on integrated circuits had doubled every year since the integrated circuit was invented. Moore predicted that this trend would continue for the foreseeable future. In subsequent years, the pace has slowed, but data density has doubled approximately every 18 months, and this is the current working definition of Moore's Law. Most experts, including Moore himself, expect Moore's Law to hold for at least another two decades."

However, many felt that changes in colleges and universities, as well as increased research and development, would be required to capture the true potential of IT to reform pedagogy and enhance SME&T learning (see Chapter 2).

CASE STUDIES OF INNOVATIVE COURSES

Professors Jean-Pierre Bayard, California State University, Sacramento (CSUS), and Ben Shneiderman, UMD, described four innovative, technology-intensive SME&T courses. They indicated that in each of these courses, currently available educational technology supported new teaching methods and enhanced undergraduate learning. The presenters' descriptions of these courses also shed light on factors that can motivate faculty and administrators to try new approaches to technology and education. Among the four courses, two came about in response to an ongoing problem of high dropouts and failure rates among students taking introductory SME&T courses. Faculty members developed the other two courses after observing that students who appeared successful in upper-level classes did not perform well afterwards, in the workplace and in subsequent classes. Both types of problems proved to be powerful motivators, encouraging individuals and groups of faculty to develop and deliver the innovative courses.

At the workshop, Bayard explained that

he had learned about innovations in pedagogy and technology while working as a fellow at the University of Wisconsin's National Institute for Science Education (NISE). NSF provided funding to Bayard and other members of the NISE "College Level One Team" to study and recommend improvements in undergraduate SME&T education, with the goal of retaining more students in these disciplines. Bayard noted that the College Level One Team initially focused on introductory courses, "what we call 'pressure points' and courses that…turn off students from science, engineering, math and technology."

Bayard said that the team used several criteria to select exemplary applications of IT that appeared to help engage and retain students in SME&T education. They sought applications of currently available technology (that could easily be adopted by other colleges and universities) across a variety of different types of undergraduate institutions. They also hoped to demonstrate that IT could help individual faculty members, departments, or institutions solve local problems. Finally, Bayard noted that they selected only those courses and programs in which IT was "transformative," helping to achieve at least one of seven principles for good practice in undergraduate education outlined by Chickering and Gamson (1987):[3]

- Encouraging student-faculty contact
- Encouraging cooperation among students
- Encouraging active learning
- Giving prompt feedback
- Emphasizing time on task
- Communicating high expectations
- Respecting diverse talents and ways of learning

Based on these criteria, the College Level One team identified nine courses, including not only introductory "pressure points," but also upper-level classes. They conducted detailed case studies of these applications of IT to SME&T education. Three of these case studies are summarized here, and all nine can be viewed at the College Level One "Learning through Technology" Web site (Millar et al., 2001).

Bayard presented two examples of innovative SME&T courses designed to increase retention and learning among first-year students. The first was an introductory college algebra course at the University of Houston-Downtown (UHD). This urban university has an open admission policy and a diverse student body. About one-third of the students are African American, one-third are Hispanic, and one-third are of other races. Many students have had negative experiences with mathematics in high school and lack basic skills. Although the university has offered a variety of remedial programs, seniors graduating in the early 1990s were overwhelmingly white. The lack of minority students successfully completing courses and moving on to graduate

_____
[3]A more recent study identified a similar list of factors affecting college success: student-student interaction, student-faculty interaction, and time on task (Astin et al., 1993).

suggests that greater efforts are needed to help all students succeed (Millar et al., 2001).

The catalyst for change at UHD was the high failure rate from introductory college algebra, averaging about 70 percent across all sections and instructors. Among those students who did pass and go on to take calculus, instructors found that few understood the core concept of a function. As a result of these problems, university faculty did not like being assigned to teach the class. At that time, most mathematics faculty followed a standard curriculum, which outlined specific mathematical skills to be taught in the introductory linear algebra class. For example, students were expected to learn how to solve a three-by-three system of equations. Instructors presented students with detailed step-by-step approaches to solving such equations, as well as other types of problems included in the curriculum. Faculty developed and pre-sented example problems, theorems, and proofs.

A group of mathematics instructors decided to try a new approach, emphasizing real-world problems, teamwork, and technology. These instructors introduced graphing calculators, both to help students visualize the concept of a mathematical function and to eliminate some of the tedious calculations. Today, students in some sections of introductory college algebra use this new approach, working with graphing calculators in small groups, where they discuss and solve problems. Bayard presented data comparing the passing rate (a grade of C or higher) in these "reformed" sections of college algebra with the rate in traditional sections, and the relative performance of the two groups in their next course (see Table 1-2).

Bayard emphasized that, although these quantitative data reveal only a modest increase in student success as a result of the

TABLE 1-2 *Outcomes of Reforms in College Algebra at University of Houston-Downtown*

Semester	Sections/Enrollment	Grade C or Better		Grade C or Better in Next Course	
		Traditional	Reformed	Traditional	Reformed
Fall 1996	Traditional: 3/75 Reformed: 6/202	38%	46%	35%	36%
Spring 1997	Traditional: 3/91 Reformed: 3/75	38%	39%	32%	26%
Fall 1997	Traditional: 3/74 Reformed: 3/51	45%	48%	20%	29%
Spring 1998	Traditional: 3/87 Reformed: 3/69	35%	51%	19%	28%

SOURCE: Bayard, 2000.

changes enabled by IT, more qualitative indicators do indicate a large change. For example, he said that students "feel a huge difference" in terms of their interest in algebra, instructors are more enthusiastic about teaching, and attendance is up. Bill Waller, one of the instructors who developed and teaches the innovative course, puts it this way (Millar et al., 2001):

> I can only give you anecdotal evidence, but the ambiance in the classroom is totally different compared to before. The biggest thing that I've enjoyed about it is when you go into the classroom, you're not dreading going. You're not thinking, How many are going to show up today? How many are going to be paying attention? Are they going to ask any questions? Am I going to get people to ask any questions? It's just a much different classroom atmosphere than before (University of Houston-Downtown, "Evidence of Success," p. 2).

Bayard's second example of innovative introductory SME&T education for first-year students was a course called "IMPULSE" (Integrated Math, Physics Undergraduate Laboratory Science, and Engineering) at the University of Massachusetts, Dartmouth (UMASSD). Because this university was formerly a technical institute, the mathematics and physics departments were happy to work with engineering faculty to create an integrated approach to teaching these subjects.

As at UHD, the catalyst for change was high failure rates, but in this case, the student population was quite different. Engineering students who were accepted on the basis of their high scores on the mathematics portion of the SAT frequently failed courses or dropped out altogether during their first year. According to Bayard, first-year students saw their required mathematics, physics, and chemistry courses as irrelevant—an obstacle they had to get through in order to reach the engineering courses they were interested in. Among those who succeeded, some found their second-year engineering courses were not what they had expected.

To overcome this problem, engage students, and retain them, an interdisciplinary team of faculty developed the IMPULSE curriculum. Students enrolled in IMPULSE attend studio classrooms, where they spend most of their time working collaboratively in teams of three to four on a variety of laboratory projects. For example, each team may be assigned to conduct and videotape a physics experiment demonstrating the motion of a projectile across the room. Using technology, students are able to capture data (such as data on the position of the projectile at various times) and record it in personal computers. Then, each team uses a computer to plot and analyze the data, answering questions about physical concepts such as velocity and acceleration.

These projects help students learn across disciplines. Conducting physics experiments helps them understand concepts in this field. At the same time, to successfully analyze the data from the physics experiments, students must apply concepts of basic calculus, such as derivatives. And, because students often must troubleshoot the equipment, they develop engineering skills, including the ability to localize problems and develop alternative solutions.

To support the understanding of these concepts developed in the studio classrooms, IMPULSE also includes mini-lectures in physics and calculus. The overall approach is borrowed from the successful "Workshop Physics" program at Dickinson College (Laws, 1997; Laws et al., 2001) and "Studio Physics" at Rensselaer Polytechnic Institute (Large, 2001).

Collaboration is central to the IMPULSE program. Engineering students work together in project teams, live together in assigned areas of the dormitory, and take many classes together. According to Bayard, students objected strongly to being forced to live with one another, and also said they found the work very hard, but nevertheless felt that the group approach "helps them a lot."

The IMPULSE program appears to have met its goal of reducing attrition. During the fall 1999 semester, students enrolled in IMPULSE earned an average of nearly 16 credit hours, or 5 credits more than the average among first-year engineering students enrolled in traditional mathematics, physics, and science classes in the fall of 1998. In addition, higher percentages of IMPULSE students successfully completed calculus and physics classes on schedule than had students in previous years, before the integrated approach was adopted (see Figure 1-1). Overall, attrition among first-year engineering students has dropped from 40 percent to 17.3 percent since the implementation of the new program (Millar et al., 2001).

Bayard's third example illuminates how

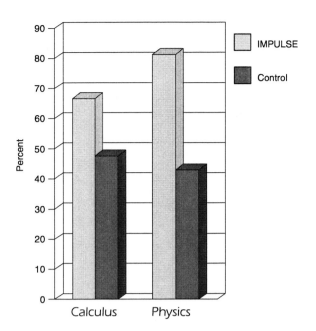

FIGURE 1-1 Percentage of first-year engineering students passing courses on schedule at UMASSD. SOURCE: Bayard, 2000.

IT can help upper-level faculty increase student learning. This example was an upper-level, elective geology course at San Diego State University (SDSU). Bayard said that Eric Frost, an associate professor at this comprehensive research and teaching university, became increasingly unhappy with his lecture-based approach in the early 1990s. Frost observed that students who performed well in the class did not really understand the underlying concepts, based on their subsequent performance in other geology classes and in the workplace. This problem led Frost to dramatically change his approach. To match this course more closely to job requirements and obtain IT resources, he worked with an oil company and the San Diego Supercomputer Center of the University of California at San Diego.

Today, instead of lecturing, Frost teaches students to find oil and gas by learning how to identify fault lines. He assigns groups of three to four students to semester-long projects in which they use data from the supercomputer to create maps. The governments of oil-rich nations sponsor some of these projects. After creating the maps, students search for fault lines, and they present their results to sponsoring partners and at scientific conferences. Frost acts as a "cheerleader and guide," spending many hours with individuals and teams as needed. Although Bayard noted that there has been no formal evaluation of this new approach, he said that the oil company now provides scholarships to Frost's students, hires them following their graduation, and moves them up the corporate ladder. Bayard joined Frost's students for one of their regular weekly lunches to discuss their projects, and saw that they were enthusiastic and shared a spirit of community.

Following Bayard's presentation of these case studies, UMD computer science professor Ben Shneiderman described his collaborative, technology-based approach to teaching upper-level undergraduate and graduate classes. Shneiderman explained that he was motivated to take this new approach during a visit to a large corporation that hires many graduates of the UMD computer science program. He reported that managers at this corporation said, "your students are great, but they don't know how to work in teams."

This problem led Shneiderman to develop a more collaborative approach to computer science education over the follow-ing two decades. He explained that this collaborative approach resulted from years of experimenting with various elements of technology and pedagogy, observing which elements were most effective, and incorporating those elements in subsequent courses. As a result of this scientific approach, Shneiderman said, his current teaching is guided by a philosophy that includes three components: Relate-create-donate (Shneiderman, 1998b). Students *relate* to each other in collaborative groups. These groups *create* ambitious projects and then *donate* them to people outside the classroom (Shneiderman, 2000).

Shneiderman said that students in his current upper-level course, Human Factors in Computer and Information Systems, have donated a variety of projects. Some students in this class have helped nursing home directors by analyzing and reporting on different strategies for teaching elderly residents how to use computers and the Internet. Another team set up a database allowing a regional charity to track donors and volunteers, and another helped a local high school develop a plan for computer usage.

As a way to encourage students in this course to relate to each other, Shneiderman has introduced "open" projects. He requires each student team to post its term-length project on the Internet and has found that this process encourages students to polish the projects and to learn more about each other's work. Near the end of the semester, each team posts its project report, and students outside the project team are assigned to review these draft reports. Students send both positive and negative comments, with a copy to Shneiderman. Each project team has three days to revise its posted report, based on comments received (Shneiderman, 1998a). The final projects are posted on the class Web site each year and are maintained on the Internet as a resource for future students (Students of Dr. Ben Shneiderman, 2000).

Acknowledging that "I was never taught this stuff," Shneiderman shared what he has learned about collaborative approaches to education. He allows students to place themselves on teams, based on short biographies that they prepare at the beginning of each class. Students sign contracts agreeing to accept responsibility as team members, and each team is supported both by specially trained teaching assistants and by Shneiderman.

Shneiderman argued that the open, collaborative approach is more successful in helping students master computer science than his past methods. He described two indications of this increased success. First, he noted that, three or four of the papers posted on the Web by student teams enrolled in his Human Factors class in 1998 included publishable results. One of the projects was accepted at an international conference, and a student presented it in Italy. By comparison, student teams enrolled in earlier Human Factors classes, who were not required to openly post and critique each others' projects, produced only one or two projects that included some publishable results (Shneiderman, 1998a).

Shneiderman said that he continues to find that three to four in every ten undergraduate student projects can be published or presented in peer-reviewed venues. Second, Shneiderman noted that one in ten student projects developed currently results in an operational computer system that is either used directly or serves as the basis for immediate development of software and hardware.

Bayard and Shneiderman provided data indicating that in these four selected undergraduate SME&T courses, technology has supported new teaching approaches and yielded positive impacts. The anecdotal and quantitative data they presented indicates that these transformed courses have had positive effects on students, faculty, employers, and the community. A summary of the positive impacts described by these two presenters is found in Table 1-3.

EVALUATION AND ASSESSMENT CHALLENGES

Workshop participants agreed that it is very difficult to evaluate the full impact of IT-enabled education reforms on students, faculty, higher education institutions, employers, and communities. Their views were similar to those participating in an earlier workshop on the uses of IT in undergraduate education, who observed that "assessment and evaluation of technology-enriched courses are in their early stages of

TABLE 1-3 *Indicators of Positive Impacts in Case Study Courses*

Program/Course	Institution	Indicators of Positive Impacts
Geological Sciences 505	San Diego State University	Increased student enthusiasm Students routinely present at conferences Students hired and promoted Graduating students offered higher salaries
College Algebra	University of Houston	Improved passing rates Increased student motivation to study math Increased attendance Increased faculty motivation, enjoyment
IMPULSE (Integrated mathematics, physics, engineering)	University of Massachusetts Dartmouth	Increased retention of first-year students Improved grades in first semester Students perceive they are working harder Students report they are learning a lot

Human-Computer Interaction	University of Maryland	Increased student motivation
		More student papers accepted at
		    conferences and by journals
		Provide IT services to university and
		    community
		Increased teacher motivation

SOURCE: Bayard, 2000, June; Shneiderman, 2000, June.

development" (Ellis, Seiter, and Yulke, 1999, p. 6).

Workshop presenters pointed to several reasons for this difficulty. First, evaluations of educational programs are usually based on analysis and interpretation of data gathered from assessments of student learning. Yet, most current assessment methods have been designed based on a more traditional view of education and evaluation. Often, undergraduate SME&T students are assessed using methods that reflect only the ability to remember facts over a short time period. In a recent review of such methods, an NRC committee (NRC, 2001a) concluded that: "most widely used assessments of academic achievement are based on highly restrictive beliefs about learning and competence not fully in keeping with current knowledge about human cognition and learning" (p. 2).

As a result, current assessment methods may be ill-suited to measuring student learning gains when faculty innovate with pedagogy and technology. For example, assessments that have been designed to measure an individual student's achievement may be difficult to apply when learning is enhanced through small group collaboration. And, although a few researchers are using computers to link ongoing assessment with instruction, many current assessments rely on paper-and-pencil methods, making them poorly aligned with learning enabled by IT (NRC, 2001a).

A key question in evaluating the impact of IT in education is whether technology-intensive approaches provide any advantage in student learning, when compared with more traditional approaches. In theory, computers are capable of providing individualized, interactive instruction, like that provided by a human tutor. Because one-on-one tutoring has been shown to increase student achievement dramatically, when compared with one instructor teaching 20 to 30 students, some experts argue that IT can yield similar gains in learning (Fletcher, 2001). The reality, however, is that most current applications of IT in U.S. classrooms do not take advantage of these capabilities. Researchers have conducted hundreds of studies that compare test scores and satisfaction of students attending classes where there is a live instructor with those of students receiving the same material via video, audio, or other technology-based delivery mechanisms. Most of these comparative studies find no significant difference in student learning with the alternative modes of education (Russell, 2001).

Two recent reviews of such comparative studies (Wisher et al., 1999; Phipps, 1999) found that most have been poorly designed. Often, investigators compared the scores of students who volunteered for technology-rich classes (and hence may be highly moti-

vated to succeed with this delivery system) with students enrolled in traditional classes. Few studies used an experimental research design, with students randomly assigned to one of the two modes of education. Another problem is that many education and training courses involve a mix of on-line and face-to-face interaction, making it difficult to separate the effects of the two modes of education. As a result of such problems, the two reviews reached similar conclusions—that most comparative studies to date yield little concrete information about the effectiveness of IT-enabled education.

Based on the assumption that education takes place when an expert teacher instructs students, most evaluations of the effectiveness of technology-rich courses have focused on delivery methods, rather than on content and learning. Ben Shneiderman, noting that his computer science students like to conduct studies focusing on delivery methods, said, "I sometimes joke that it is like we have a running experiment to see whether the strawberries delivered by trucks or strawberries delivered by cars are fresher or better in some way."

The second, more fundamental difficulty in evaluating innovative applications of IT to transform SME&T education relates to goals. Workshop participants noted that until there is a greater consensus about the goals of higher SME&T education, it may be difficult to conduct evaluations that would be widely accepted.

The first step in evaluating any program is to define the program's goals. However, administrators, faculty, students, and parents have varying short-term and long-term goals. For example, some SME&T faculty may feel that, currently, the most important goal is to retain students within their chosen discipline. However, others may believe that the most important goal of undergraduate education is to create a group—possibly quite small—of highly qualified graduates, with complete mastery of specific content areas. This goal is reinforced by the strict prerequisite structures in many SME&T undergraduate programs. At the workshop, Jean-Pierre Bayard highlighted the tension between this goal and the goal of retaining more students. He contrasted the success of the IMPULSE program in retaining first-year engineering students with his perception that many engineering schools view high dropout rates among first-year students as a mark of success in eliminating people who would not become successful engineers.

In addition to faculty and administrators, others involved in undergraduate SME&T education have varying goals. Some students and their parents may care little about formal evaluations, but place high value on the future career success that might result from innovative educational programs. Employers may be most concerned about the ability of colleges and universities to prepare students to perform in the workplace, caring less about student grades or program evaluations.

Given the problem of varying goals, Christopher Dede suggested applying a variety of evaluation methods to influence different audiences to adopt, develop, or de-

mand innovative, technology-rich education. Many SME&T faculty, as well as outside funding agencies that support development of educational technology, will require rigorous quantitative evaluations. On the other hand, informal evaluations, including personal testimonials from faculty and examples of student work, might help influence some faculty to consider using new, technology-rich approaches. Bayard and others involved in the Learning through Technology project have gathered these types of informal evaluations, including "hallway conversations" with faculty who are using IT, and have made them available on the Internet (Millar et al., 2001).

Workshop participants acknowledged that IT not only supports new educational approaches that may be difficult to evaluate, but also provides new opportunities for assessment and evaluation (NRC, 2001a). When students interact with educational software, that software can be designed to collect detailed records of student activities that provide information about student learning. Medical professor Ron Stevens (University of California at Los Angeles [UCLA]) presented one such approach. Stevens originally developed the IMMEX (Interactive Multimedia Exercises) program for medical students, and it has been modified for use in Los Angeles-area elementary and secondary schools. Although IMMEX is not currently used in undergraduate SME&T education, the program illustrates the potential benefits of embedding ongoing assessment into instruction.

Stevens was originally motivated to develop IMMEX because he saw that multiple-choice examinations failed to fully assess the skills required of future medical doctors. Today, IMMEX is being used in middle schools and high schools to help students learn to solve problems and measure changes in students' problem-solving abilities. Extensive professional development is provided to teachers, who play a central role in helping students use the interactive software. Meeting in teams under the guidance of UCLA researchers, teachers create conceptual problems for students. Each problem has 50 to 60 variants, allowing students multiple opportunities to practice solving problems that use a variety of types of resources and data. The software tracks the steps the students take in solving the problems and uses pattern recognition to categorize each student's strategy. Teachers can use the tracks of individual student performance to assess progress and to compare a student's individual progress with that of his or her peers. These tracks can also help teachers to refine instruction, feedback, and coaching. The information can also be provided directly to students, allowing them to think about how to improve their own performance.

Stevens noted that a full evaluation of IMMEX, or any other program, should be multidimensional, including assessment of student learning, curriculum, and teaching practice. Chapter 2 outlines possibilities for such multifaceted approaches to evaluation.

CULTURAL AND INSTITUTIONAL CONSTRAINTS

Over the past decade, some policy makers, educators and members of the public, have questioned the quality of U.S. higher education. In response, individual colleges and universities, as well as educational associations have launched efforts to improve undergraduate teaching and learning (American Association of Universities, 2001; Project Kaleidoscope, 1991, 1998). Experts have called on colleges and universities to tap the power of IT as they undertake such efforts (Boyer Commission, 1998; NRC, 1999d). However, despite these reports and activities, workshop participants observed that transforming undergraduate SME&T education with IT is a slow and difficult process. This is because faculty, administrators, students, parents, and employers are required to adopt new goals and assume unfamiliar roles (see Table 1-1).

Workshop presenters observed that widespread diffusion of innovative undergraduate courses, such as those they described, might be constrained by the current culture and institutions of undergraduate SME&T education. For example, Shneiderman noted that he is the only one among 38 professors in his computer science department at the UMD who uses collaborative, learner-centered approaches. Bayard said that other faculty at SDSU see Eric

15

Frost as unusual, and not necessarily as a model to be followed. Commenting on Frost's new, project-based approach to learning, one participant noted: "I think we have all heard of these kinds of gems.... Usually they get sealed off by the rest of the institution, because they say, 'that is [effective] because of that particular person.'"

Three types of constraints—institutional expectations, cultural factors, and technological constraints—could potentially prevent innovative, IT-enabled approaches from being implemented on a larger scale. First, many colleges and universities reward and recognize faculty based on more "traditional" conceptions of research and teaching. Workshop participants, most of whom were mid-career or senior-level faculty, noted that they enjoyed secure, tenured positions, allowing them the freedom to use IT in new ways. However, given the competitive reality of academic science, mathematics, and engineering today, younger faculty members are motivated by, and preoccupied with, the goal of obtaining tenure. To achieve this goal, younger faculty must devote so much time to research and publishing in peer-reviewed journals that they may be unable to devote attention, time, and energy to fundamentally restructuring their teaching.

Christopher Dede asserted that some elite universities view publishing papers in refereed journals as the primary measure of success for younger faculty. If these views are correct, then current institutional reward systems, emphasizing publications,[4] may well constrain young faculty who not only want to improve their teaching, but also want to do so by using IT to transform their educational approach. In addition, as illustrated by the IMPULSE example, these new approaches to teaching often involve collaboration among faculty as well as students, including collaboration across academic disciplines. Christopher Tucker noted that it is extremely difficult to try to place articles in peer-reviewed journals, and be awarded tenure, based on truly interdisciplinary collaboration.

Time availability may constrain faculty members from adopting new approaches to pedagogy and technology. SME&T faculty who use IT to create active learning environments typically find themselves spending more time with students. In describing Eric Frost's activities at SDSU, Bayard noted that Frost works with these students "a lot more than just the three hours a week that some of us are familiar with." Elias Deeba, one of those who developed and now teaches the algebra course at UHD, has said, "Using technology, my own workload, of course, has increased tremendously" (Millar et al., 2001). Some SME&T educators may be unwilling to move toward these IT-enabled approaches if the increased workload leaves less time for research or other professional or leisure activities.

---

[4]As discussed further below, some administrators may be reluctant to base tenure or other rewards on teaching quality because of a lack of good measures of teaching quality.

Institutional expectations about faculty time could potentially constrain development of technology-rich SME&T courses, as well as their delivery. At UHD, faculty members are not expected to spend extensive time doing research, because the university sees its main mission as teaching. Reflecting this focus, faculty members are required to teach four courses per semester. This large teaching load adds to the office hours during which faculty are expected to be available for consultations with students. These teaching demands make it difficult to find time for faculty collaboration and design of new curricula. Without the grant from UHD's Teaching with Technology Learning Center, which offered release time, the professors who incorporated IT into the algebra course would not have been able to develop their new approach (Millar et al., 2001).

Technological constraints could also slow the use of IT to transform traditional undergraduate SME&T courses into more active learning environments. At the most basic level, not all colleges and universities have access to current technology. As illustrated in the UHD example, outside funding is often essential to provide the hardware and software that students and faculty need. These inequities in access to technology at the undergraduate level are somewhat similar to the broader problem in homes and elementary and secondary schools. Educational consultant Martha Darling expressed her concern about the possibility of a growing "digital divide," between the rich, who have ready access to advanced technology at home and school, and the poor, who often lack such access.

Funding to purchase and install hardware and software, by itself, will not overcome this problem. Student learning can be enabled by IT systems only when those systems work. For example, at the time Jean-Pierre Bayard visited the IMPULSE studio classrooms at UMASSD, technological problems prevented students from videotaping the physics experiments. This problem illustrates the importance of having adequate technical support staff when implementing IT-enabled approaches. The teams of computer science students enrolled in Shneiderman's classes at the UMD are supported not only by specially trained teaching assistants, but also by dedicated technical support staff. Many higher education institutions may be unable to provide this level of support. In addition, some SME&T faculty outside computer science departments may lack the expertise needed to integrate IT into design and delivery of new forms of education.

Cultural factors influence the willingness of SME&T students and faculty to embrace new technology and new forms of pedagogy. On the positive side, undergraduates who have grown up with video games and home Internet access may welcome technology-intensive approaches to education. University of Arizona mathematics professor Deborah Hughes Hallett pointed out that "today's students are powerful and fluent and agile in technology in ways that their elders are often not. This...is a powerful boost to education." On the other hand, those students who have not had access to advanced tools may be at a decided disadvantage in a technology-rich classroom.

The changing approaches to education outlined in Table 1-1 engage students in active learning, often in collaborative groups. Although one might think that students would be eager to respond to these "learner-centered" forms of education, not all students are. Shneiderman noted that every semester, he encounters one or two students who are reluctant to participate in group projects. At UHD, mathematics instructors have found that some students, who either dropped or failed the more traditional sections of introductory algebra, complain that "I've had this course before, and this is not the way it's supposed to be done" (Millar et al., 2001).

Although workshop participants noted that all of these cultural and institutional constraints currently slow widespread transformation of undergraduate education, these constraints could possibly be reversed in the future. For example, high-quality, interactive software that supports individualized instruction and learning of SME&T disciplines might be widely available. In this case, a single professor could support learning among a large, lecture-sized group of students, without spending hours with each student. In such a future, faculty and administrators would likely welcome the use of IT and the time savings that would result. The next chapter summarizes some participants' views about the future of undergraduate education, including the role of IT. The chapter also describes participants' suggestions about ways to use IT more effectively and capture its full potential to enhance learning among SME&T students.

2

Planning for Uncertainty

A FRAMEWORK OF GIVENS AND UNKNOWNS

Information technology (IT) is changing at a breathtaking pace, making it virtually impossible to accurately predict its future impact on teaching and learning in undergraduate science, mathematics, engineering, and technology (SME&T) education. As Philip Agre of the University of California, Los Angeles Department of Information Studies put it, "everyone knows that IT is going to change the world, but nobody knows how." Agre went on to say that, although no one can predict the future, it is possible to prepare. After discussing many examples of current uses of IT in undergraduate SME&T education on the first day of the workshop, during the second day, participants looked toward the future. To facilitate this process, Alan Schwartz from

PolicyFutures[1] led workshop participants through the first phase of a multiple scenario-planning exercise, designed to help prepare them for future possibilities.

Schwartz launched the exercise with three examples of how different organizations ended up planning for the "wrong" future. His first example was the U.S. Army's decision to build a large fleet of Abrams M1A1 tanks in the late 1970s. Designed to fight the Soviet army on the plains of Europe, the tanks are heavily shielded for protection against Soviet shells. They are so heavy that a military plane can carry only one at a time. This design, based on outdated assumptions about where battles would be fought and what the enemies' capabilities would be, has proven ill-suited for more recent battles. During Desert

---

[1] A consulting firm that provides strategic planning, scenario planning, and policy forecasting services to public and private clients.

Storm in the early 1990s, when rapid deployment was important, it took fully 6 months to deploy the Abrams tanks. In addition, another aspect of the tanks' design—night vision that was superior to that of the enemy—allowed the tanks to avoid enemy attack during Desert Storm, making the heavy armor superfluous.

A second example of misdirected planning, based on the assumption that the future would resemble the past, was the creation of the Alaska Natural Gas Transportation Institute in 1977, to tap the natural gas that is found in the oil fields on Alaska's North Slope. At that time, when experts were predicting oil prices would reach $200 per barrel, parts of the pipeline were built, but after oil prices dropped, it was never completed. (With oil prices now rising, it is possible that the pipeline will be built someday; nevertheless, it is clear that the plans made in 1977 were not appropriate to the future that developed over the following two decades.)

Schwartz's final example was the U.S. automobile industry in the 1960s, which believed that Americans would always love big cars, that gasoline would continue to be plentiful, and that reliability wasn't an issue because Americans traded in their cars every two years. Because U.S. auto makers acted based on this prevailing wisdom, Japanese firms were able to capture a large share of the U.S. market with smaller, more reliable, and more fuel-efficient cars in the 1980s.

To further illustrate his point that one cannot reliably plan for an uncertain future

TABLE 2-1 *Changing Benchmarks*

Benchmark	1990	2000
Number of Web Pages	0	Millions
Dow Jones Industrial Average on January 3	2,810	11,358
Soviet Union	Exists	Does not exist

SOURCE: Schwartz, 2000.

by simply extrapolating from current trends, Schwartz presented data on dramatic technological, economic, and political changes that have taken place over the past decade (see Table 2-1).

Schwartz suggested that an important step in planning for an uncertain future is to make a list of relevant events and to categorize the events as certain or uncertain to continue into the future. (For example, the Abrams tank was designed because the army felt that the existence of the Soviet Union was a certainty.) Schwartz maintained that this process of categorizing events can allow one to identify signposts that might be monitored to indicate how the future is unfolding. He led the workshop participants in brainstorming to identify factors influencing development of technologies that: (1) might be useful in science and mathematics education, and (2) might influence implementation of those technologies over the next 10 years. Using the resulting list, participants then assembled in small groups to discuss which factors they felt were certain and which were uncertain.

Next, the small groups assembled in a plenary session, compared their lists, and created a framework of certain and uncertain factors that are likely to influence the course of IT in SME&T education over the next decade (see Table 2-2).

Had this session been a full multiple-scenario planning exercise, the participants would have been led to develop a framework for looking at the future based on the list of issues, and to identify signposts that might be used to monitor how the future unfolds. The framework and signposts could then be used by decision makers to build strategies for dealing with an uncertain future. Despite the lack of such a full framework, workshop participants suggested several strategies. Presenters and discussants suggested that the following steps could help to overcome the cultural and institutional constraints to change discussed in chapter 1.

STEPS TOWARD DIFFUSION OF INNOVATIONS IN PEDAGOGY AND TECHNOLOGY

Steps for Educators and Researchers

Several workshop presenters suggested that the first, and most important, step that SME&T faculty might take would be to adopt a more "scientific" approach to improving SME&T education. For example, Shneiderman emphasized the importance of establishing the overriding goal of the course or program at the outset. Based on this goal, a faculty member could then formulate a hypothesis about what educational approaches and/or technologies are most likely to achieve this goal, and develop a protocol for evaluating progress toward the goal. Shneiderman suggested testing the hypothesis by experimenting with alternative educational delivery methods and learning processes.

Experts in the wider community, as well as those attending the workshop, are calling for a more rigorous, scientific approach to development of new educational approaches (Anderson, Greeno, Reder, and Simon, 2000; National Research Council [NRC], 2001b). Educators and researchers who adopted this approach would continually evaluate and refine their approach to teaching and learning. They would base their evaluations on assessments of student learning gains and might also assess learning among faculty and instructors involved in innovative courses. This process would help educators and researchers to identify those educational approaches that have been shown to enhance student learning. Policy makers might focus educational funding on these approaches for maximum effectiveness (Lyon, 2001).

At the workshop, Dede called for a new "culture of assessment and evaluation, where professors are willing to try new things, and view their own work critically." This requires putting time and energy into multilayered evaluation of teaching and learning, including the following steps:

TABLE 2-2 *Factors Influencing SME&T Education and IT over the Coming Decade*

Certainties	Uncertainties
Information flood	Bandwidth cost
Entertainment	Whether the IT tools needed to improve SME&T education will exist, and, if so, what they will cost
Retirement of faculty	
Demographics	Universal access
Need for learner outcomes	Student preparation for undergraduate SME&T
Structure of universities will change	Economic disparities between rich and poor students and institutions
Multiple technologies to reach millions	Business shifts high technology abroad
Scientific developments outside the United States	State funding of institutes of higher education
Price of educational commodities will drop	Whether quality mentoring will be available to all students
Universities will lose monopolies	
Learning is social	The roles of traditional higher education institutions and new, for-profit education providers
Student awareness of own skills	
Changed role of public funding	What does certification look like?
Globalization	Foreign reaction to U.S. dominance
Human pride	Whether technology can foster deep communities
Moore's Law	
Lifelong learning	Role of assessment
	Will there be believable evidence of impact on outcomes?
	Economy
	Tenure policy
	Who will bear the costs of learners? One possibility is development of new cost-sharing mechanisms, such as "educational maintenance organizations," modeled on HMO's
	Direction of change in new institutional arrangements
	Cultural attitudes towards innovations in SME&T education
	Professional values

• Gather multiple indicators of student learning. Although evidence of the benefits of IT-enabled innovations in SME&T education is growing, Dede said that "tough" assessments are needed to demonstrate that the new educational paradigm really enhances student learning. These multiple indicators may include data gathered by the instructors of courses as well as data obtained by outside evaluators.

• Assess student motivation by measuring the amount of time that students spend on projects, courses that they take over time, attendance, and retention. IT can help to do this, by providing logs of student interactions with a course or Web site.

• Include both quantitative and qualitative measures (which may require using more than one external evaluator).

• Focus on formative assessment[2] of student learning and, if possible, aggregate to summative. Formative assessment will provide the information on how the project worked, which is essential for improvement and replication of the project. The National Institute for Science Education (NISE) provides resources for assessment

through its Field-tested Learning Assessment Guide (FLAG) Web site (NISE, 2001).

• Match evaluation methods to the intended audience. For example, Martha Darling noted the need to demonstrate that the innovations "work" to end-users of the education system, including employers.

• Focus assessment on students' intellectual products and learning processes, rather than on technology.

As one part of this scientific approach to SME&T education, faculty might collaborate across disciplines to develop new courses as well as to evaluate and refine courses they have already created. Ongoing assessment, evaluation, and revision of courses would lead to new findings about effective approaches. Several workshop participants suggested that SME&T educators collaborate to create new interdisciplinary journals focusing on pedagogy and technology. The journals would provide a place where the results of this ongoing research could be published and widely shared.

Steps for Higher Education Institutions

Commenting on the innovative courses described by Bayard, one participant likened the situation in higher education to that of consumers and businesses faced with the possibility of purchasing innovative technology. He recommended that faculty and

---

[2]Assessments are typically used for a variety of purposes. Nevertheless, many experts distinguish between *formative* assessments, used primarily to guide instruction and learning, and *summative* assessments, used primarily to determine whether a student has attained a certain level of competency after completing a particular phase of education (NRC, 2001a).

administrators read *Crossing the Chasm* (Moore and McKenna, 1999; see also Rogers, 1982), which describes why high technology products typically are never widely adopted by the general public. He said the book argues that individuals fall onto a normal curve, with "early adopters" (who are technically literate) on one end and "laggards" at the opposite end. The problem, he said, is that individuals in the middle of the bell curve are unlikely to adopt high technology without incentives and rewards.

As a first step toward bridging the "chasm" between early adopters of technology and the majority of other SME&T faculty, workshop participants suggested that colleges and universities try to increase the majority's knowledge about both IT and new approaches to education. Dede and other presenters identified several ways in which institutions might do this:

• Help faculty learn about the potential of collaborative, learner-centered educational approaches. Colleges and universities might consider involving groups of faculty (both in person and in virtual learning communities) in shared learning about the new approaches.

• Support cross-disciplinary collaboration to develop and implement innovative, IT-enabled approaches.

• Provide financial and other support for student and/or faculty projects that provide service to the university and/or to the community.

However, as illustrated in Moore's book, knowledge alone is unlikely to lead to widespread innovation, unless it is supported by recognition and concrete rewards for faculty who take advantage of professional development opportunities to restructure their teaching. Colleges and universities could publicly recognize excellent teaching that incorporates IT. Shneiderman noted that the University of Maryland recognizes innovators by inviting them to give public presentations on successful uses of IT. Outside organizations, too, might grant recognition. One workshop participant suggested that the U.S. Department of Education provide awards and recognition for faculty who are exemplary in their uses of IT to enhance student learning.

Several presenters and participants called on higher education institutions to evaluate and reward SME&T faculty, based not only on their research, but also on the quality of their teaching. Some suggested basing tenure, salaries, sabbaticals, and other employment decisions on indicators of teaching quality, as well as research. These indicators might include publications in new journals focusing on pedagogy, peer review by master teachers, the number of publishable papers produced by students, and employers' views of graduates. However, these suggestions may be difficult to implement, because many faculty and administrators question the validity, fairness, and reliability of currently available methods for assessing teaching quality.

Steps for Public and Private Research and Development

At the workshop, Christopher Dede presented a videotape made by a private firm to market its concept for a future form of human-computer interface. He also showed another vendor's videotape, in which people wore wireless computing devices and interacted with "smart objects" in an office where computers are embedded in the walls and furniture. Dede noted that these products, envisioned by a few innovators in private firms, have the potential to enhance human communication and learning. However, he said that there is a wide gap between these early prototypes and what private firms actually develop. Dede argued that, because most private research currently focuses on using IT for information exchange rather than for communication, public funding is essential in order to develop uses of IT that enhance learning.

Workshop participants emphasized that the National Science Foundation (NSF) has played an essential role in supporting and financing the kinds of innovations in SME&T education that were discussed at the workshop. The NSF's role has included analyzing, and disseminating information about, current innovations. For example, Bayard's case studies of applying IT to undergraduate education were part of a year-long NSF project on "Improving Learning through Technology." As one outcome of that project, these case studies are now easily accessible via the project's Web site (Millar et al., 2001). In 1999, NSF organized a workshop to share experiences and define future priorities for the use of IT in undergraduate SME&T education (Ellis et al., 1999), and NSF supported the National Academies' workshop summarized here.

Research and development funding from the NSF also was critical to developing the innovative undergraduate courses discussed at this workshop. To cite just one example, in 1992, University of Houston-Downtown (UHD) was selected to host summer workshops on the writing and use of interactive texts as part of a project funded by NSF and IBM. Through these workshops, mathematics faculty gained access to hardware and software that could be used to teach algebra, and also learned about new approaches to mathematics. At about the same time, the NSF-supported Harvard Calculus Consortium began publishing a series of textbooks (e.g., Hughes Hallett and Gleason, 1999), which gave legitimacy to the innovative approaches being developed by UHD mathematics faculty. Finally, in addition to this new knowledge and technology, NSF provided the critical grant that supported the three instructors' release time while they developed the new curriculum (Millar et al., 2001).

Despite such successes, several workshop participants wondered whether innovations in technology and pedagogy could spread more widely, across departments and institutions, without additional, and larger-scale, funding. Andries van Dam asserted that the NSF typically funds educational technology research in $100,000 grants over one or two years, and argued that these amounts were insufficient.[3] He noted that some workshop participants had mentioned costs of about $1 million to produce a single course "using today's technology." Van Dam called for larger amounts than this, over a sustained period, to support the long-term research needed to develop and implement tomorrow's technology.

Van Dam suggested that SEMATECH, a consortium of semiconductor manufacturers supported by both member companies and federal funds, might provide a useful model for long-term research and development. SEMATECH was created as a nonprofit organization by 14 U.S. firms in 1987, and the following year, Congress appropriated $100 million annually for 5 years to the new group, matching the companies' contributions. Originally organized to develop procedures for manufacturing next-generation computer chips, SEMATECH soon began to emphasize strengthening the smaller firms that supply the chip manufacturers with equipment. Acting as a communication channel, SEMATECH helped the chip makers define their needs and supplier companies develop the capabilities to meet those needs. These efforts succeeded in helping U.S. firms gain a larger share of the global computer chip market in the early 1990s, and the federal government continued funding SEMATECH beyond the origi-

nal 5 years. However, since the mid-1990s, the organization has chosen to eliminate all federal support in order to open its membership to foreign firms and increase its flexibility (NRC, 1999c).

Jack Wilson described a current initiative that provides smaller investments designed to help diffuse innovation based on currently available technology. At Rensselaer Polytechnic Institute (RPI), he and other faculty and administrators have begun to make institutional reforms, focusing on three key elements of undergraduate education: computing, communication, and cognition. As described by Wilson, RPI chose to follow a "scientific" approach, first establishing goals, then testing alternative ways to reach those goals "in a way that would allow you to continuously refresh and change." RPI's innovations—particularly replacing most large lectures, recitations, and laboratory sections with studio classrooms—have been so successful that RPI received an $8.8 million grant from the Pew Charitable Trusts. The Pew Learning and Technology Program, housed at RPI, is currently using these funds to provide financial and technical support to other institutions that wish to "undertake substantial systemic change." Wilson emphasized that the new program does not simply provide funding, but also works actively with institutions to ensure that IT is used in ways that reduce costs and enhance learning (Bartscherer, 2001).

Whether through new partnerships or through existing methods, public and private funding agencies could support indi-

---

[3]The NSF has awarded much larger grants for educational technology in the past, ranging up to nearly $1 million over two years in one case.

vidual faculty and higher education institutions as they take a scientific approach to deploying IT in undergraduate SME&T education. In this approach, researchers start by establishing the goals of the educational program. They build assessment into the instructional program from the start, and revise curriculum and delivery methods on an ongoing basis, based on data about student learning and achievement of other program goals. (Examples can be found in NRC, 2001a.)

Workshop participants generally agreed that the focus of research, development, and demonstration should be on student learning and quality of instruction, rather than on any particular technological tools. Nevertheless, some participants called for increased investments in research and development of particular technologies. First, Christopher Tucker noted that private firms are rapidly deploying broadband networks for business and residential customers, yet little is known about the educational potential of these networks. He said that the growing availability of broadband raises fundamental questions about how best to tap its potential to enhance learning. For example, in traditional approaches to education, an instructor (whether in person or online) initiates the process by presenting some information to the learners. Tucker raised the question of whether, in a broadband education system, the learner would receive a "story line" or lecture to begin the learning process. He noted that another possibility would be to create learning systems that would be entirely self-selected or self-guided, leaving open the question of which approach might be more effective at enhancing learning.

Second, Tucker noted that new generations of intelligent browsers can allow faculty and students to transcend current digital databases which replicate academic disciplines. For example, the American Economic Association produces one such database, EconLit. With further research and development, these new browsers might support interdisciplinary collaboration to enhance faculty and student learning. Third, Dede noted that virtual reality technology is moving very quickly. His research has established that for certain types of SME&T subject matter, modeling and visualization in virtual reality can be very powerful in enhancing student learning (Dede, Salzman, Loftin, and Sprague, 1999). Dede stressed the need for funding to support further research that would examine how best to use this technology for educational purposes.

CONTINUING THE DIALOGUE

Many workshop presenters and participants expressed a desire for ongoing collaboration with others interested in developing innovative, effective approaches to undergraduate SME&T education. They noted the importance of continuing to learn about, and from, innovations in education and technology in both the public and private sectors. Some workshop participants expressed a desire to learn more about the ways in which particular educational tools (such as those listed in Appendix A) might support the innovative approaches to pedagogy discussed at the workshop. Their concerns suggested a need to create an ongoing forum for exchange of information. With support from the U.S. Department of Education, the NRC Center for Education initiated such a forum in late 2000, the Improving Learning with Information Technology (ILIT) Project. Although this project is focused on elementary and secondary education, its activities and findings are likely to guide innovations in pedagogy and technology in higher education as well.

The ILIT project is designed to create an ongoing community of experts in technology, cognitive science, and education who are devoted to improving education through creative applications of information technology.[4] These experts will work to develop a path toward improving teaching and learning in elementary and secondary schools through the use of IT. The overall project is designed to enable educational decision makers to make rational and strategic decisions about how they purchase and use education technology. Just as SEMATECH helped supply firms better understand the needs of the chip makers to whom they sold, the ILIT project seeks to empower the education community to drive the development of hardware and software tools that meet the needs of children and educators alike. A final project goal is to help guide the federal research agenda in the relevant areas.

---

[4]Further details on the project, including contact information, are available at: http://www4. nationalacademies.org/cfe/cfe.nsf. Click on "Organizational Structure and Projects," and on "Improving Learning with Information Technology." [July 9, 2001].

References

American Association of Universities. (2001). Assessing Quality of University Education and Research: Project Description. Available: http:www.aau.edu/issues/AQdescript.html. [October 23, 2001].

Anderson, J.R., Greeno, J.G., Reder, L.M., and Simon, H.A. (2000). Perspectives on Learning, Thinking, and Activity. *Educational Researcher, 29*(4), 11-13.

Astin, A.W. (1993). *What matters in college? Four critical years revisited.* San Francisco: Jossey-Bass.

Bartscherer, P. (2001). *The Pew Learning and Technology Program.* Available: http://www.center.rpi.edu/PewHome.html. [May 28, 2001].

Bayard, J.P. (2000, June). What's out There: Instructional Technology for College-Level STEM Instructors. Presentation at National Research Council Workshop on the Roles of Information Technology in Improving Teaching and Learning in Undergraduate Science, Mathematics, Engineering and Technology Education, held in Washington, DC, June 20-21.

Boyer Commission on Educating Undergraduates in the Research University. (1998). *Reinventing undergraduate education: A blueprint for America's research universities.* Menlo Park, CA: Carnegie Foundation for the Advancement of Teaching.

Chickering, A.W. and Gamson, Z.E. (1987). Seven Principles for Good Practice in Undergraduate Education. American Associate for Higher Education Bulletin 39(7), 3-7.

Dede, C. (2000). Emerging Influences of Information Technology on School Curriculum. *Journal of Curriculum Studies, 32*(2), 281-304.

Dede, C., Salzman, M., Loftin, B., and Sprague, D. (1999). Multisensory Immersion as a Modeling Environment for Learning Complex Scientific Concepts. In W. Feurzeig, and N. Roberts (Eds.), *Computer modeling and simulation in science education.* New York: Springer-Verlag.

Ellis, A., Seiter, D., and Yulke, S. (1999). *Workshop on improving undergraduate education in the mathematical and physical sciences through the use of technology: Preliminary report.* Madison, WI: University of Wisconsin, Wisconsin Center for Educational Research. Available: http://www.wcer.wisc.edu/teched99/report.htm. [May 23, 2001].

Felder, R.M. (1993). Reaching the Second Tier—Learning and Teaching Styles in College Science Education. *Journal of College Science Teaching, 22*(5), 286-90.

Felder, R.M. (1996). Matters of Style. *American Society for Engineering Education Prism 6*(4), 18-23.

Fletcher, J.D. (2001). Evidence for Learning from Technology-Assisted Instruction. In H.F. O'Neil and R. Perez (Eds), *Technology applications in education: A learning view*. Hillsdale, NJ: Erlbaum Associates.

Godleski, E. (1984). Learning Style Compatibility of Engineering Students and Faculty. In *Proceedings, Annual Frontiers in Education Conference. American Society for Engineering Education/Institute of Electronics and Electrical Engineers*, Philadelphia, PA.

Hake, R. (1998). Interactive Engagement Versus Traditional Methods: A Six-Thousand Student Survey of Mechanics Test Data for Introductory Physics Courses. *American Journal of Physics, 66,* 64-75.

Hanna, D.E. (2000). *Higher education in an era of digital competition: Choices and challenges*. Overland Park, KS: Atwood Publishing.

Hilosky, A., Sutman, F., and Schmuckler, J. (1998). Is Laboratory-Based Instruction in Beginning College-Level Chemistry Worth the Effort and Expense? *Journal of Chemical Education, 75*(1), 100-104.

Hughes Hallett, D. and Gleason, A. (1999). *Calculus: Second edition*. New York: John Wiley and Sons.

International Technology Education Association. (2000). *Standards for technological literacy: Content for the study of technology*. Reston, VA: Author.

Johnson, D.W., Johnson, R.T., and Smith, K.A. (1998). Cooperative Learning Returns to College: What Evidence is there that it Works? *Change, 30*(4), 27-35.

Laws, P.W. (1997). A New Order for Mechanics. In J.Wilson (Ed.), *Proceedings of the conference on introductory physics course*. New York: John Wiley and Sons, Inc.

Laws, P.W., Braught, G., Buchan, G., Greenbaum, S., Oliver, G., and Ward, D. (2001). *Workshop physics/activitybased physics*. Available: http://physics.dickinson.edu/Physic...p_Physics/

Workshop_Physics_Home.htm/. [May 21, 2001].

Large, A. (2001). *Physics phlats: Home of studio physics I*. Available: http://www.rpi.edu/dept/phys/Courses/studio_physics/physI/physImain.html/. [May 21, 2001].

Leonard, G.B. (1968). *Education and ecstacy*. New York: Dell Publishing Company.

Lyon, G. R. (2001, March 8). Measuring Success: Using Assessments and Accountability to Raise Student Achievement. Statement of Dr. G. Reid Lyon, Chief, Child Development and Behavior Branch, National Institute of Child Health and Human Development, National Institutes of Health. Subcommittee on Education Reform, Committee on Education and the Workforce, U.S. House of Representatives. Washington, DC.

Macdonald, R.H. and Korinek, L. (1995). Cooperative Learning Activities in Large Entry-Level Geology Courses. *Journal of Geoscience Education, 43,* 341-345.

McDermott, L.C., Shaffer, P., and Somers, M. (1994). Research as a guide for curriculum development: An illustration in the context of the Atwood's machine. *American Journal of Physics, 62,* 46-55.

Millar, S., Bayard, J., Ehrmann, S., Jungck, J., McMartin, F., Molinaro, M. (2001). *Learning through technology* Web site. Available: http://www.wcer.wisc.edu/nise/cl1/ilt/default.asp/. [May 21, 2001].

Moore, G.A. and McKenna, R. (1999). *Crossing the chasm: Marketing and selling high-tech products to mainstream customers*. New York: HarperBusiness.

National Council of Teachers of Mathematics. (2000). *Principles and standards for school mathematics*. Reston, VA: Author.

National Institute for Science Education. (2001). *Field-tested learning assessment guide*. Available: http://www.wcer.wisc.edu/nise/cl1/flag/start/. [May 5, 2001].

National Research Council. (1996). *National science education standards*. National Committee on Science Education Standards and Assessment. Washington, DC: National Academy Press.

National Research Council. (1999a). *How people learn: Brain, mind, experience and school*. Committee on Developments in the Science of Learning, J.D. Bransford, A.L. Brown, and R.R. Cocking (Eds.). Washington, DC: National Academy Press.

National Research Council. (1999b). *How people learn: Bridging research and practice*. Committee on Learning Research and Educational Practice, M.S. Donovan, J.D. Bransford, and J.W. Pellegrino (Eds.). Washington, DC: National Academy Press.

National Research Council. (1999c). *Funding a revolution: Government support for computing research*. Committee on Innovations in Computing and Communications: Lessons from History. Washington, DC: National Academy Press.

National Research Council (1999d). *Transforming undergraduate education in science, mathematics, engineering, and technology*. Committee on Undergraduate Science Education. Washington, DC: National Academy Press.

National Research Council. (2001a). *Knowing what students know: The science and design of educational assessment*. Committee on the Foundations of Assessment, J. Pellegrino, N. Chudowsky, and R. Glaser (Eds.). Washington, DC: National Academy Press.

National Research Council. (2001b). *Science, evidence, and inference: Report of a workshop*. Committee on Scientific Principles in Education Research, L. Towne, R. Shavelson, and M. Feuer, (Eds.). Washington, DC: National Academy Press.

National Science Foundation. (2000). *Science and engineering indicators*. Washington, DC: Author. Available: http://www.nsf.gov/sbe/srs/scindoo/start.htm. [May23, 2001].

Phipps, R. (1999). *What's the difference? A review of contemporary research on the effectiveness of distance learning in higher education*. Washington, DC: The Institute for Higher Education Policy.

Poole, B.J. and Kidder, S.Q. (1996). Making Connections in the Undergraduate Laboratory. *Journal of College Science Teaching, 26*(1), 34-36.

Project Kaleidoscope. (1991). *What works. Leadership: Challenges for the future. Volume II*. Washington, DC: Author.

Project Kaleidoscope. (1998). *Shaping the future of undergraduate science, mathematics, engineering and technology education: Proceedings and recommendations from the PKAL day of dialogue*. Washington, DC: Author.

Rogers, E.M. (1982). *Diffusion of innovation*. New York: McMillan.

Russell, T.L. (2001). *The no significant difference phenomenon: A comparative research annotated bibliography on technology for distance education*. Montgomery, AL: International Distance Education Certification Center.

Schwartz, A. (2000, June). How to think about the future; looking at certainties and uncertainties, forces and drivers. Presentation at National Research Council Workshop on the Roles of Information Technology in Improving Teaching and Learning in Undergraduate Science, Mathematics, and Technology Education, held in Washington, DC, June 20-21.

Seymour, E., and Hewitt, N.M. (1997). *Talking about leaving: Why undergraduates leave the sciences*. Boulder, CO: Westview Press.

Shneiderman, B. (1998a). Educational Journeys on the Web Frontier, *EDUCOM Review, 33*(6), November/December. Available: http://www.educause.edu/ir/library/html/erm9861.html. [July 5, 2001].

Shneiderman, B. (1998b). Relate-Create-Donate: A teaching/learning philosophy for the cyber-generation. *Computers & Education, 31*, 25-39.

Shneiderman, B. (2000, June). Pedagogic Strategies for Applying Educational Technology: Relate-

Create-Donate. Presentation at National Research Council Workshop on the Roles of Information Technology in Improving Teaching and Learning in Undergraduate Science, Mathematics, Engineering and Technology Education, held in Washington, DC, June 20-21.

Shneiderman, B. (2000). *Relate-Create-Donate*. Available: http://www.cs.umd.edu/hcil/relate_create_donate. [July 5, 2001].

Springer, L., Stanne, M.E., and Donovan, S. (1997). *Effects of small-group learning on undergraduates in science, mathematics, engineering, and technology: A meta-analysis*. Madison, WI: National Institute for Science Education.

Students of Dr. Ben Shneiderman. (2000). *Student HCI online research experiments*. Available: http://www.otal.umd.edu/SHORE2000/. [July 5, 2001].

Tobias, S. (1992). *Revitalizing undergraduate science: Why some things work and most don't*. Tucson, AZ: Research Corporation.

Watson, S.B. and Marshall, J.E. (1995). Effects of Cooperative Incentives and Heterogeneous Arrangement on Achievement and Interaction of Cooperative Learning Groups in a College Life Science Course. *Journal of Research in Science Teaching, 32*(3), 291-299.

Web-Based Education Commission. (2000). *The power of the internet for learning: Moving from promise to practice*. Report to the President and the Congress of the United States. Available: http:// www.webcommission.org. [May 21, 2001].

Wisher, R., Champagne, M., Pawluk, J., Eaton, A., Thornton, D., and Curnow, C. (1999). *Training through distance learning: An assessment of research findings*. Alexandria, VA: U.S. Army Research Institute.

Wright, J.C. (1996). Authentic Learning Environment in Analytical Chemistry using Cooperative Methods and Open-Ended Laboratories in Large Lecture Courses. *Journal of Chemistry Education, 73*(9), 827-832.

Appendixes

Appendix A

Workshop Background Paper: Excerpts from a Document Prepared by the Committee on Information Technology

BACKGROUND: THE COMMITTEE ON INFORMATION TECHNOLOGY IN UNDERGRADUATE SCIENCE EDUCATION

The Committee on Information Technology in Undergraduate Science Education was organized in December, 1995 and completed its work in November of 1999. The committee's charge was to improve undergraduate science education through the use of information technology. Nicholas Turro of Columbia University chaired the committee. Committee members included: Stephen Ehrmann, American Association for Higher Education; Bernard Gifford, Academic Systems Corporation; Steven Gilbert, American Association for Higher Education; B. James Hood, University of Central Arkansas; Deborah Hughes Hallett, University of Arizona; John Jungck, Beloit College; Stephen Lerman, Massachusetts Institute of

Technology; Ronald Stevens, University of California at Los Angeles; and Jack Wilson, Rensselaer Polytechnic Institute. Committee members who served limited terms included Linda Chaput, Interactive Sciences, (December, 1995— October, 1996); Stephen Hurst, University of Illinois at Urbana-Champaign (February, 1996—November, 1999); C. Bradley Moore, Ohio State University (December, 1995—April, 1997); Dorothy Stout (February, 1996-November, 1999); and James Whitesell, University of Texas at Austin (May, 1997—November, 1999).

Nancy Devino served as Staff Officer to the committee from December, 1995 through February, 1999. Jay Labov served as Staff Officer from March, 1999 until the committee completed its work in November, 1999. Other staff included: Gail Pritchard, Research Associate; Terry Holmer, Project Assistant; Stacy Lucas, Consultant; Steven Olson, Editor; and James Lawson, Editor.

APPENDIX A: TABLE OF CONTENTS

TRANSFORMING PEDAGOGY

INTRODUCTION

Information technology (IT) has dramatically transformed scientific practice in the last 50 years. The ability to handle massive amounts of data, collect data continuously in extraordinarily fine detail, perform millions of computations per second, visualize information in three and four dimensions with rotations and translations, and simulate immensely complex phenomena with multivariate, multidimensional models has become commonplace. Computers are ubiquitous in scientific workplaces, whether in offices, laboratories, or field settings. Electronic preparation of manuscripts has allowed professionals greater control over layout, graphics, and symbols, such that many now use publishers as distributors rather than as editors, layout specialists, or typesetters. The World Wide Web, faxes, and e-mail allow scientists, mathematicians, and engineers to collaborate on a daily basis over long distances and across many time zones. New technologies allow scientists to control and collect real-time data from distant locations with expensive, highly specialized research instruments.

This information technology revolution also has changed the undergraduate learning environment. Students are as likely to "surf the Web" from their dormitory rooms or teaching laboratories as they are to visit a library. They know that a portable computer or handheld calculator can perform almost all of the calculations expected in exams or problem sets. Having used computers extensively in high school, some students now arrive at college already knowing how to enter and analyze scientific data in spreadsheets and statistical graphing packages. Many more students who enter college are comfortable using these tools for a variety of other purposes.

Reflecting these changes, many faculty members have begun to post lectures and reading lists on the Internet, create on-line discussion groups, and to use IT in other ways to deliver courses. However, to be truly effective, information technology needs to be *embedded* in instruction, not just provided as an additional activity to a standard course or program. For example, in several science, mathematics, engineering, and technology (SME&T) disciplines, professors and instructors are using more than one technological innovation to help students learn. Earth scientists employ geographic information systems (GIS), global positioning systems (GPS), and remote sensing. When teaching calculus classes, some faculty use information technology to emphasize multiple representations of mathematical ideas (symbolic, verbal, numerical, and graphical) and realistic problem solving. Graphing calculators and spreadsheets have made numerical and graphical representations easily accessible to undergraduate and precollege students. This means that most students—though not yet all faculty—expect technology to be part of a mathematics classroom (see Box A-1).

However, the challenge to rethink the mathematics curriculum has just begun. The emergence of calculators that can do symbolic manipulation (computer algebra systems, or CAS) will push faculty and administrators to consider which topics in algebra and calculus they need to teach with pencil and paper—even though machines can do them—because pencil and paper

develop understanding. In addition, faculty need to learn how to use computer algebra systems to promote understanding. Can they be used to illuminate topics that students have in the past learned by rote, without much understanding? Mathematicians, scientists, engineers, teachers, and educational researchers will need to reach a consensus on such questions.

Both the power and widespread availability of these new technological capabilities, and recent scientific findings about how people learn are forcing science, mathematics, and engineering faculty members to rethink what and how they teach. Many have begun to use new pedagogical practices. The committee found that IT can play a particularly effective role in supporting six such practices:

- visualization
- simulation
- real-world problem solving
- collaboration
- inquiry
- design.

The following section describes current technological tools that enable and support each of these pedagogical practices.

CURRENT PRACTICES

Visualization

Computers are powerful tools to help

learners visualize, simulate, and construct objects in the created or natural worlds. Improvements in technology and significant decreases in the price of high-end computers mean that molecular modeling workstations now can be bought for as little as $2,000 compared to ten or more times that much only several years ago. Molecular modeling offers science educators a vehicle for helping students understand difficult abstract concepts. For example, students often have difficulty understanding the relationship between the macroscopic appearance of a substance, its symbolic representation as a chemical formula, and its molecular shape and structure as predicted by quantum mechanics (Gabel, 1990). Talley (1973) documented student difficulties in understanding the particulate nature of matter and proposed three-dimensional visualization to overcome the problem. Technology offers a way to move beyond static two-dimensional representations of three-dimensional phenomena into a format that more closely simulates reality. Current molecular modeling software can alternate images of a given object at rates approaching thousands of times per second, creating a realistic three-dimensional effect. The rapid increase in computer processing speeds means that software developers now are producing pedagogical software that was mere fantasy not long ago. While the full impact and influence of this technology on science education are not yet known, preliminary results are encouraging. Williamson and Abraham (1995), for example, developed computer animations using molecular mod-

eling images. They found that students who used these tools developed better conceptual understanding of phenomena such as diffusion of intermolecular forces than did students who received conventional instruction.

Molecular modeling also can improve the linkage between lecture and laboratory. Crouch, Holden, and Samet (1996) described an innovative instructional sequence in which students learn about nucleophiles and electrophiles in a lecture, construct electron density maps of assigned compounds using molecular modeling software, and then use these maps to predict the outcome of the laboratory experiment they are about to undertake.

In contrast to visualization tools that exploit the computational capabilities of up-to-date computers, a GIS uses powerful information databases to construct detailed, precise computer maps. According to the U.S. Geological Survey,[1] "a GIS is a computer system capable of assembling, storing, manipulating, and displaying geographically referenced information (i.e., data identified according to their locations)." A GIS works by relating information from different sources for the same location. Different kinds of data in map form can be entered into a GIS, and a GIS can also convert existing digital information into maps. There are numerous GIS applications in wide-

---

[1]Available: http://info.er.usgs.gov/research/gis/title.html. [7/25/01].

spread use in many different fields, including:

- Agriculture (crop monitoring; land use management; commodity forecasting; soil studies; irrigation planning; and water resource assessment);
- Environment (pollution, weather, and climate monitoring; cause-effect studies; landscape assessment; conservation planning; and biodiversity libraries);
- Health care (asset management; ambulance routing and mobilization; epidemiological studies; and road traffic accident analysis); and
- Local government (planning and building control; land searches; boundary change modeling; property and highways maintenance; crime analysis; natural disaster management; and police and fire service command and control).

This list, while not exhaustive, illustrates the range of disciplines that can be expanded and deepened with GIS technology. According to the U.S. Geological Survey, an active GIS market has resulted in lower costs and continual improvements in hardware and software components. Thus, GIS tools that only recently were restricted to use by professional scientists and engineers, are now becoming part of undergraduate science and engineering programs and courses.[2]

These developments are likely to result

---

[2]Available: http://www.ehr.nsf.gov/EHR/DUE/web/ate/atelist.htm#geos. [7/25/01].

---

in much wider GIS application in both the public and private sectors, which in turn will pressure higher education institutions to provide instruction in this kind of learning to science and engineering students. This example also indicates how information technology costs can be shared among the public and private sectors to everyone's benefit.

Many other visualization tools are finding a place in the postsecondary SME&T curriculum (see Box A-2). Spreadsheets and graphing calculators are now widely used for mathematical modeling. Large databases of all types of images are accessible to students and faculty from all over the world. The National Library of Medicine's Visible Human Project contains thousands of digitized cryosection photographs, magnetic resonance images (MRI), and transverse computerized tomography (CT) images, which together comprise anatomically correct, three-dimensional representations of the male and female human body. Although used heavily in clinical medicine and biomedical research, these images also are used widely in undergraduate courses. The Visible Human World Wide Web site[3] lists dozens of applications of the image data sets, most of which were developed by and are used at colleges and universities around the country. Other databases contain images taken by the Hubble Space Telescope of planets, stars, asteroids, and comets,[4] which can be downloaded for use in astronomy courses. Digitized video can help students understand the physics involved in sporting events (e.g., pole-vaulting), transportation (a plane take-off), and nature (river flow).

Technologies that rely on interactivity with the World Wide Web are still developing and hold promise as yet another avenue for pedagogical change. Small Java applets[5] make it possible for a Web page user to perform interactive animations, immediate calculations, and other simple tasks without having to send a user request back to the server. Wolfgang Christian at Davidson College has created a Web site with numerous Java applets for physics, which he calls Physlets.[6]

The array of computer-based visualization tools available can dramatically affect not just how postsecondary SME&T educators teach their courses, but how they select the topics to cover.

Simulation

Simulations let students view multiple aspects of complex systems simultaneously or sequentially. For example, an ecosystem or an architectural development can be constructed from many components with various connections of material and energy flow. Output data can be displayed in scatter plots, histograms, pie charts, and on maps concurrently and can be linked so that all representations change simultaneously when variables are manipulated. Similarly,

[3]Available: http://www.nlm.nih.gov/research/visible/visible_human.html. [7/25/01].

[4]Available: http://www.jpl.nasa.gov/pictures/. [7/25/01].

[5]Java is a programming language expressly designed for use in the distributed environment of the Internet. It was designed to have the "look and feel" of the C++ language, but it is simpler to use than C++ and enforces a completely object-oriented view of programming. Java can be used to create complete applications that may run on a single computer or be distributed among servers and clients in a network. It can also be used to build small application modules (known as applets) for use as part of a Web page. Applets make it possible for a Web page user to interact with the page. (Available: http://www.whatis.techtargetcom/. [7/25/01].

[6]See http://WebPhysics.Davidson.Edu/Applets/Applets.html. [7/25/01].

BOX A-3 Features and Advantages of Simulations

- encourage student ownership of a research or problem-solving agenda;
- allow students access to large, complex data sets;
- allow students to conduct the same experiment multiple times;
- draw on multidisciplinary learning, such as mathematics, in scientific exploration;
- help students develop quantitative skills as they engage in successive rounds of hypothesizing and logical and numerical testing of hypotheses;
- require interpretation of multiple representations of data;
- provide novel experiences each time the simulation is run;
- offer flexibility in classroom contexts (e.g., case studies, investigative labs, homework, distance education, local context, background and talents of students and teachers); and
- allow the use of many tools at once.

SOURCE: The BioQUEST Curriculum Consortium, available at http://bioquest.org/. [7/25/01].

---

a transformation of the data (e.g., to log-log scales) can be reflected in all displays in a linked manner.[7] Picture a situation where students are collaborating with each other or with research scientists from remote sites and are able to illustrate alternative graphical and iconic representations of the same data to highlight patterns in that data. The integration of simulations with real-world data allows the learner to incorporate both theoretical and empirical data to understand a complex phenomenon.

Many simulations have been constructed to help students learn long-term research strategies. These micro worlds engage students in the exploration of open-ended problems and complex data sets, giving them numerous modes and opportuni-

ties for data analysis, visualization, and the ability to explore multiple variables using tools from many disciplines. Simulations allow students to investigate contemporary research problems, explore "what-if" questions, pose new problems, and examine fundamental concepts and classical experiments. These learning environments are content- and process-rich, since these types of simulations are open to such diverse manipulation for long periods of investigation. These elaborate simulations help students learn which tools are appropriate in which contexts and why one tool is more powerful than another in a given context.

Several features of currently available simulation tools offer advantages to faculty interested in enhancing student mastery of scientific and technical disciplines. These features and advantages are listed in Box A-3.

Because of these features and advan-

---

[7]For example, see BioQUEST, available at http://bioquest.org/. [7/25/01].

BOX A-4 Examples of Simulation Practices

The Virtual Genetics Lab at the University of Pittsburgh offers a course in conjunction with an honors course in genetics, and the **NextStep-based simulator** completely replaces lab experiments. At James Madison University, a **four-year integrated science and technology (ISAT) curriculum** examines issues and scientific content in biotechnology, energy, environmental issues, information and knowledge management, and manufacturing. Students use the computer as a productivity tool, simulator, model builder, laboratory, and communication medium to concentrate on the connections between science and the technology rather than disciplinary differences.

tages, simulations probably will play an increasingly important role in undergraduate SME&T classrooms and laboratories. For example, in some fields, certain experiments may be too risky for novices to perform, they might be too advanced for a student's laboratory skills, or the necessary equipment might be too costly. Another possibility is that conducting a real-world experiment would require more time than is available in a course (e.g., multiple crosses or crosses of organisms with long breeding cycles in a genetics experiment). Simulations are a reasonable alternative (see Box A-4). However, wet labs offer an indispensable experience to students that often can-

not be replaced by the use of information technology.

Simulations can provide critical support for education based around realistic problem solving, such as the programs described earlier. By linking to research databases, simulations may enhance data mining[8] and, in some cases, allow students to do original, open-ended research. Using simulations, students can replicate aspects of historically important models and classical experiments. They also can learn long-term strategies of scientific research using strategic simulations. Finally, simulations are a means of enhancing conceptual integration and conceptual change.

Real-World Problem Solving

Our society faces challenges that were unknown to our parents and grandparents. Increases in global atmospheric carbon dioxide may be linked to a gradual warming of the planet. Run-off of fertilizers used to grow crops and fecal waste from livestock can contaminate drinking water supplies hundreds of miles away. The safety of the food supply, the advantages and disadvantages of genetic testing, and the development of reproductive technologies to benefit infertile couples all pose difficult

---

[8]Data mining is the analysis of data for relationships that have not previously been discovered. Data mining results can include forecasting or simply discovering patterns in the data that can lead to predictions about the future.

challenges to society. The solutions to these problems will be as complex and multifaceted as the problems themselves and will draw on a wide range of expertise.

Providing opportunities for students to develop their problem-solving skills is becoming a high priority for postsecondary science and engineering educators. Faculty members, departments, and institutions are recognizing the value of constructing contemporary science curricula around real-world problems. Institutions that require science credits for graduation have led the development of many courses for non-specialists organized around modern scientific problems. In some cases a semester or year-long course is composed of interchangeable modules of different topics, such as water quality (e.g., the Modular Chemistry Consortium based at University of California-Berkeley[9]); global warming (e.g., Workshop Physical Science[10]), and environmental decision-making (e.g., The BioQUEST Curriculum Consortium[11]). Publishers have responded with textbooks and other educational resources that emphasize problem solving, including those with a multidisciplinary approach (Trefil and Hazen, 1995) and those with a disciplinary emphasis (Schwartz et al., 1997).

Focusing SME&T courses on real-world problems will not only encourage faculty members to develop sophisticated and realistic assignments for students, but also will introduce students to a variety of information technology tools. Information technology can play a critical role in helping faculty develop real-world problems, and in helping students search among many possible solutions. The Internet provides access to a wide range of contemporary scientific problems and potential solutions. Students can tap into vast amounts of unfiltered information, including large databases, images of objects of all types and sizes, and textual information (some of which is available in print, and which may or may not be peer reviewed). As they seek solutions to real-world problems, SME&T students can connect with one another, with their instructors, and with practicing professionals. Learning from scientists, mathematicians, and engineers in industry and in government (e.g., National Aeronautics and Space Agency, Environmental Protection Agency) will be crucial, since they tend to be at the cutting edge of the field and know about the most promising solutions. These experts in the field can help a student understand a complicated, interdisciplinary scientific problem, in ways that were impossible only a few years ago (see Box A-5).

Collaboration

Scientific research often involves extensive collaboration among colleagues. Single-author papers are increasingly unusual in scientific and mathematical journals. Similarly, manufacturing relies on

---

[9]Available: http://mc2.cchem.berkeley.edu. [7/25/01].

[10]Available: http://Physics.Dickinson.edu. [7/25/01].

[11]Available http://Bioquest.org/. [7/25/01].

BOX A-5 Examples of Problem-Solving Practices

In a "**collaboratory**" for undergraduate research and education students at Evergreen State College, connect in real time to instruments at research facilities, such as national laboratories, and use data collected by these instruments to solve problems posed by the professor on their home campus.

In the BioCalc program at the University of Illinois, special sections of **Calculus & Mathematica** for life science students use the same computer tools as the traditional sections, but include problems of interest to biology students such as carbon dating, population modeling, and the kinetics of drug clearance in the body.

Real-world problems are the focus of **Physics of Energy and the Environment**, a course for non-science majors at the University of Oregon. After learning about energy, electricity, and fossil fuels, students spend a week exploring the effect of human activity on the ozone layer and global warming. (Available: http://zebu.uoregon.edu/1997/phys161.html.). [7/25/01].) Click on 1999 Course.

The **BioQUEST Library** is a compendium of computer-based tools, simulations, and textual materials that supports collaborative, research-like investigations in biology classrooms. For example, *Evolve* is a computer simulation that allows users to model evolution experimentally by controlling a number of variables. including the starting population size, overall population size, intensity of natural selection, pattern of inheritance, and proportion of migration in a hypothetical population. (Available: http://www.apnet.com/bioquest/.) [7/25/01].

Harvey Mudd College has a nationally recognized **clinic program** centered on a multidisciplinary design-oriented approach to real-world problems. The computer science, engineering, mathematics, and physics departments sponsor about 40 "clinic projects" annually in which students work in groups of four or five under the guidance of a student team leader, a faculty advisor, and a liaison from the sponsoring organization. A 1996-1997 clinic was sponsored by BHK Enterprises, a local Southern California supplier of lamps for scientific and industrial use. The BHK clinic involved research to discover and design an improved deuterium plasma arc source. This clinic required students to acquire a fundamental understanding of, and the skills to model, the mechanisms of gaseous excitation and emission, as well as empirical design based on student measurements. (Available: http://www.hmc.edu/acad/clinic/.) [7/25/01].

teams of designers to create new products, as do software companies to write code for a software application. Postsecondary institutions also need to provide students the opportunity to participate in collaborative projects in which they can develop and nurture their teamwork skills using modern information technology as a tool.

Information technology can offer all students the opportunity to learn teamwork skills, including students who live off campus. These students often have full-time jobs in addition to family responsibilities. Without access to information technology and telecommunications, they would be at a distinct disadvantage to their on-campus peers. But students need not be limited to virtual interactions on the World Wide Web. Collaborative projects also can involve more discrete team activities such as the development of a CD-ROM. The first of the three examples in Box A-6 is a project designed to develop both information technology and teamwork skills.

Inquiry

Recent changes in science, mathematics, and technology education at the K-12 level promise to have a profound impact on postsecondary education. National standards in mathematics (National Council of Teachers of Mathematics, 1989), science (American Association for the Advancement of Science, 1993; National Research Council [NRC], 1996b), and technology (International Technology Education Association, 2000) have been developed and are being adopted and translated by state departments of education. In the not-too-distant future, high school students will begin arriving at college with very different learning experiences and expectations (NRC, 1999b).

For example, the *National Science Education Standards* (NRC, 1996b) emphasize inquiry as a means of learning fundamental scientific concepts. Inquiry is defined in the Standards as "a set of interrelated processes by which scientists and students pose questions about the natural world and investigate phenomena" (NRC, 1996b, p. 214). When engaging in inquiry, students construct explanations, test those explanations against current scientific knowledge, and communicate their ideas to others. They identify their assumptions, use critical and logical thinking, and consider alternative explanations. In this way, students actively develop an understanding of science by combining factual scientific knowledge with reasoning and thinking skills.

College courses historically have consisted of lecture, recitation, and laboratory. However, this configuration, and particularly the lecture, may contribute little to some students' learning. Standard physics lectures do not help most students grasp fundamental concepts (McDermott, Shaffer, and Somers, 1994). Birk and Foster (1993) compared student grades in large multi-section lecture courses and found that the experience and lecturing skills of the instructor did not correlate with student achievement in the course. Although Birk and Foster conceded that results could be attributed to a mismatch between the instructor's goals and the assessments used to determine student grades, they maintained that the lecture method is not the best learning tool for most students. For these reasons, students who have been exposed to inquiry-based learning in their K-12 education could be frustrated by many of the prevailing postsecondary SME&T pedagogical practices, particularly at the introductory level.

Unfortunately, the laboratory component of many undergraduate SME&T courses also can be less than optimal in developing students' conceptual understanding. The experiments and activities in these courses are often structured in such a way that students can perform the actions step-by-step and achieve the predetermined outcome to within a small margin of error (if they are careful). Students may answer questions that are drawn from the preparatory information at the beginning of the activity and fill in the lab report at the end—yet still leave the laboratory with very little understanding of what was supposed to be learned (Poole and Kidder, 1996). Even in "newer" reform-minded curricula, laboratory experiences often are self-contained, emphasize verification of established conclusions, and do not correlate with material presented in subsequent instructional sessions (Hilosky, Sutman, and Schmuckler, 1998).

Inquiry as defined by the above standards, and "extended inquiry" in which students undertake real scientific research projects extending over several days or weeks, present major pedagogical challenges to their instructors. In the process of investigating a scientific question, both students and educators are required to use such diverse skills as the following (Tinker, 1997):

- modes of thinking, including posing good questions and developing experimental strategies;
- procedural skills, such as data collection and instrument calibration;
- familiarity with design and construction (safety procedures or machine shop skills); and
- analytical techniques, such as graphing, mathematical modeling, and statistics.

Although most scientists with doctoral degrees acquire the skills listed above during completion of their dissertation research, they may not feel qualified to teach them. They also may feel constrained by department-wide curricula and the need to cover a specified range of topics for students to enroll in subsequent courses. Faculty time also can be a factor when considering the effort necessary to develop or modify laboratory activities (for which professional recognition or rewards are often minimal). Another barrier to the kinds of reform advocated by the NRC (1996a, 1999b) and the National Science Foundation (NSF) (1996) is the presence of faculty members with master's degrees who have not conducted an extended research project. An additional problem is that beginning graduate students, who have little experience with extended inquiry projects, are often employed as teaching assistants and lead laboratory classes.

An increasing number of academic institutions are beginning to integrate computers into introductory science and engineering courses. In the traditional lecture/recitation/laboratory system, computers have been used as aids for demonstrations in lectures, to run simulations, in microcomputer-based laboratories, and for out-of-class problem solving. This initial practice often encourages even more ambitious technology-based projects such as the use of Calculus & Mathematica,[12] Workshop Physics

(Laws, 1991, 1999), and Studio Physics (Wilson, 1994).

Technology now provides exciting new opportunities for learners to conduct their own investigations of real problems (see Box A-7). In addition to working with data generated or collected by others, information technology enables students to collect and analyze their own scientific data without regard to time or place. Commercially available computer-interfaced sensors can measure almost any phenomenon, and they can be used with handheld calculators, battery-operated computer-based laboratory interfaces, and personal data assistants, making them opportune for fieldwork.[13] In experiments not suited for computer-based data collection, technology still can allow learners to manipulate and analyze data, fit data to known mathematical equations, rapidly analyze large data sets with sophisticated statistical tests, simulate with models, and draw conclusions based on the outcomes of these processes. Students may even have access to "real" sensors used by scientists, such as devices for measuring the temperature of a lava flow or obtaining water samples as a function of depth. With modern networking, these instruments that collect data may be a world away from the students.

---

[12]Available: http://www-cm.math.uiuc.edu/. [7/25/01].

[13]See The Concord Consortium for further information about sensors and other uses of information technology in education. Available: http://www.concord.org/. [7/25/01].

Principles of Global Dynamics at the University of North Carolina, Chapel Hill, is a quantitative study of the earth system as a whole, from the core to the upper atmosphere. The course provides a global view of the planet and describes modern approaches to monitoring the earth, its interior dynamics, and its external environment. An important feature of the course is an electronic document that follows the contents of the course and allows students to complement and expand the information by following hyperlinks to Web sites selected for the course. One section of the course teaches students explicitly how to access, filter, and use a wide array of electronic resource materials. Finally, a separate electronic discussion forum is available to students, so that they may post comments, e-mail their homework, and notify their classmates and instructors of interesting data or links found. Montana State University offers a **course for certified K-12 teachers** to learn how to use the Internet to teach mathematics and science in the context of earth system science. This course investigates the relationships among changes in the atmosphere, ocean circulation patterns, and environmental processes both on and below the earth's surface. From the Internet, curricular materials and resources designed by "Network Montana Project Earth System Science" serve as model lessons to teach aspiring teachers how to integrate concepts with image processing and analysis techniques for their own future instructional environments. In the **Concepts of Physics** program at Kansas State University, non-specialists, including prospective elementary school teachers, pose questions about physical phenomena and use interactive digitized video to obtain answers.

Design

Computer-aided design (CAD), once exclusively the domain of professional engineers, is now used in undergraduate engineering courses as early as the freshman year. Although CAD bears a superficial resemblance to simulations—they both attempt to reproduce real phenomena graphically—CAD is only one step on the pathway to designing and manufacturing a real product. Growing numbers of engineering schools are offering CAD instruction, because it provides important workplace skills. For example, many professional engineers now use AutoCAD, a high-quality design tool. Even some high school students are now learning to use these tools (Ercolano, 1998).

As distance education and collaboration between individuals at different sites become more common, the use of design tools that can be transmitted over the Internet will likely increase. Designers can build a sequence of visual images into Web settings, and a user can view, move, and rotate those images, as in the example found in Box A-8.[14]

_____

[14]Available: http://whatis.techtargetcom/vrml.htm for definition of VRML. [7/25/01].

APPLICATIONS OF IT ACROSS SME&T DISCIPLINES

Many of the six pedagogical practices described above can be incorporated into courses that traditionally have not had a strong information technology component. In addition to the examples presented above, information technology is central to many other current efforts to improve teaching and learning in undergraduate SME&T fields. Table A-1 provides additional examples of innovative pedagogical practices, organized by discipline.

ASSESSING STUDENT LEARNING

Currently, the dearth of effective instruments for measuring the effectiveness of new teaching and learning approaches that incorporate IT poses a tremendous barrier to the diffusion of these new approaches. Evaluation instruments must allow for metrics that the science and engineering teaching community are willing to accept. Some educators who resist curricular change argue that, until standardized tests such as the Graduate Record Examinations and Medical College Admission Test change their orientation to emphasize analysis of information, the solution of open-ended problems, and design of experiments to test hypotheses, using information technology to transform undergraduate education cannot succeed.

To make progress, pioneering faculty members will need to become actively involved with changing these tests. Although developing student learning assessments to correspond with new pedagogical methods can be extremely challenging, it can be done. For example, a group of chemistry professors at the University of Wisconsin-Madison felt strongly that their "structured active learning" (SAL) approach in introductory chemistry resulted in increased student learning. However, their colleagues were reluctant to embrace it. Consequently, faculty members from the science, engineering, and mathematics disciplines and on-campus experts in assessment and statistics

TABLE A-1 *Examples Highlighting Pedagogical Practice Innovation*

Discipline	Example	Pedagogical Innovation
Earth and Space Science		
Astronomy	Project CLEA Gettysburg College http://www.gettysburg.edu/project/physics/clea/CLEAhome.html. [7/25/01].	• Visualization Laboratory exercises use digital data and color images to illustrate modern astronomical techniques.
Geography	The Geographer's Craft University of Texas at Austin http://www.colorado.edu/geography/gcraft/contents/html. [7/25/01]. (The Geographer's Craft pages have moved to the University of Colorado.)	• Visualization • Real-World Problem Solving Students address research problems with "appropriate" geographical concepts and techniques drawn from cartography, geographic information systems, remote sensing, spatial statistics, and other information technologies.
Geology	"An Integrated, Computer-Assisted Approach to Teaching Introductory Geology Laboratories" University of Illinois, Urbana-Champaign http://www.geology.uiuc.edu/HTML. Click on: SHurst, fieldtrips [7/25/01].	• Visualization • Simulation Electronic geology field trips
Life Science		
Biology	BioQUEST Curriculum Consortium Beloit College http://www.bioquest.org. [7/25/01].	• Simulation • Real-World Problem Solving • Collaboration Publishes *The BioQUEST Library:* a collection of simulations for learning long-term research strategies; tools, data sets, and modeling.
	Workshop Biology University of Oregon http://biology.uoregon.edu/Biology_www/workshop_biol/wb.html. [7/25/01].	• Simulation • Real-World Problem Solving • Collaboration Epidemiology, demography, and cardiac physiology simulations published in *The BioQUEST Library*.
Immunology	IMMEX University of California at Los Angeles http://www.coled.umn.edu/edutech/immex/. [8/8/01].	• Real-World Problem Solving Artificial neural networks that distinguish novice and expert strategies during complex problem solving.

continued

TABLE A-1 *Continued*

Discipline	Example	Pedagogical Innovation
Physical Science		
Chemistry	ChemLinks Beloit College http://chemlinks.beloit.edu/. [7/25/01]. Modular Chemistry Consortium University of California, Berkeley http://mc2.cchem.berkeley.edu/. [7/25/01].	• Visualization • Simulation • Real-World Problem Solving • Collaboration • Inquiry Applications of technology include multimedia components for illustrating concepts through simple simulations, animations, and video clips; World Wide Web-based literature searching; MathCAD-based problem solving; molecular modeling; graphical representations of large data sets with Quick Time movies; and a few modules with large-scale interactive multimedia components.
	New Traditions University of Wisconsin http://newtraditions.chem.wisc.edu/. [10/3/01].	• Visualization • Simulation Curriculum project for undergraduate chemistry includes MathCAD-based interactive texts for physical chemistry; ChemScape, a multimedia encyclopedia of lab techniques to free instructor time and facilitate distance learning; CyberProf, an integrated, easy-to-use system for delivering course material through the Web; and molecular modeling exercises.
	Molecular Science Initiative University of California Los Angeles http://server2.nsic.ucla.edu/ms/. [7/25/01].	• Visualization • Simulation • Collaboration Development and implementation of a fully digital and network-deliverable molecular science curriculum, including WebCT for developing sophisticated Web-based environments, Calibrated Peer Review software, Mastering Chemistry tutorial software, and multimedia "Exploration" tools.

TABLE A-1 *Continued*

Discipline	Example	Pedagogical Innovation
Physics	Workshop Physics Dickinson College http://physics.dickinson.edu/Physics Pages/Workshop_Physics/Workshop_ Physics_Home.htm. [7/25/01].	• **Visualization** • **Real-World Problem Solving** • **Collaboration** • **Inquiry** Activity-based real-time data acquisition and analysis; design of the curriculum is informed by outcomes of physics education research.
	Studio Physics Rensselaer Polytechnic Institute http://www.rpi.edu/dept/phys/studio_ physics/phys1/phys1main.html. [10/3/01].	• **Visualization** • **Real-World Problem Solving** • **Collaboration** • **Inquiry** Computers are used for the acquisition and analysis of data, which can be collected either from sensors or digitized video.
	The Center for Science and Mathematics Teaching Tufts University http://ase.tufts.edu/csmt/. [7/30/01].	• **Real-World Problem Solving** • **Collaboration** • **Inquiry** The Center develops curricula, activities, and computer tools that allow students to participate actively in their own learning and to construct scientific knowledge for themselves. Using these materials, the students learn directly from the physical world. The Center's substantial conceptual-learning research and evaluation program guides the development of materials.

Mathematics

	Calculus & Mathematica University of Illinois, Urbana-Champaign Ohio State University http://www-cm.math.uiuc.edu/. [10/3/01].	• **Visualization** • **Real-World Problem Solving** Lectureless virtual courses using a symbolic algebra package for calculus education in a computer lab context.
	Calculus, Concepts, Computers and Cooperative Learning (C4L) Purdue University http://www.math.purdue.edu/~ccc/. [10/3/01].	• **Visualization** • **Real-World Problem Solving** • **Collaboration** Use of Interactive SET Language, an interpreted mathematical programming language closely resembling the language of sets and functions and Mathematica for calculus.

continued

Discipline	Example	Pedagogical Innovation
	Harvard Calculus Consortium Harvard University http://www.math.harvard.edu/. [10/3/01].	• Visualization • Real-World Problem Solving Extensive use of graphing calculators for visualization, numeric modeling, and problem solving.
	Project CALC: Calculus as a Laboratory Course Duke University http://www.math.duke.edu/education/ proj_calc/. [10/3/01].	• Visualization • Real-World Problem Solving Real applications and complex data modeled with computer packages such as MathCad, Mathematica, and Maple.
	Calculus from Graphical, Numerical, and Symbolic Points of View St. Olaf College http://www.stolaf.edu/people/zorn/ ozcalc/index.html. [10/3/01].	• Visualization • Real-World Problem Solving Single variable and multivariable calculus explored with extensive use of graphics and computational environments.
	Workshop Mathematics Dickinson College http://www.workpage.com/ f/84/546f.htm. [10/3/01].	• Visualization • Real-World Problem Solving • Collaboration • Inquiry Introductory mathematics that takes advantage of recent research findings in mathematics and science education and makes effective use of new computer technologies.
	Calculus in Context Smith College http://www.math.smith.edu/Local/ cicintro/cicintro.html. [7/25/01].	• Visualization • Real-World Problem Solving Use the method of successive approximations to define and solve problems, develop geometric visualization with hand-drawn and computer graphics, while giving numerical methods a more central role.

TABLE A-1 *Continued*

Discipline	Example	Pedagogical Innovation
Engineering	Engineering Academy of New England University of Connecticut, University of Massachusetts-Amherst, University of Massachusetts-Lowell, University of Rhode Island, and Hartford Graduate Center http://www.egr.uri.edu:80/ne. [10/3/01].	• Simulation • Real-World Problem Solving • Collaboration • Design Modern communications technologies enable collaboration between five engineering and technology education programs and their respective industrial partners to produce a set of engineering courses, curricula, and workforce training programs. Information technology-based curriculum projects feature interactive multimedia tools for simulating the manufacturing design process.
	The Gateway Engineering Education Coalition Columbia University, Cooper Union, Drexel University, New Jersey Institute of Technology, The Ohio State University, Virginia Polytechnic University, and University of South Carolina http://www-gateway.vpr.drexel.edu. [10/3/01].	• Simulation • Real-World Problem Solving • Collaboration • Design Multimedia computer-aided instruction tools have been developed for introductory and intermediate materials engineering courses. A major thrust of the coalition's work is a collection of collaborative educational technology and methodology projects that facilitate sharing of data, information, and resources among member institutions.
	Southern California Coalition for Education in Manufacturing Engineering (SCCEME) California State University–Fullerton, California State University–Long Beach, California State University–Los Angeles, University of California–Irvine, University of California–Los Angeles, and University of Southern California http://www.csulb.edu/colleges/coe/main/index.html. [10/3/01].	• Visualization • Simulation • Collaboration Member institutions are developing a variety of hypermedia-based instructional modules covering modern methods and new technologies for manufacturing to be used in campus-based engineering courses and workplace-based training programs. This effort includes development of a "Simple Authoring Environment" for cross-platform, rapid development of hypermedia educational materials.

were recruited to assess learning by students emerging from either the traditional introductory chemistry course or the SAL course. The faculty members used their own criteria and instruments to see if they could distinguish the two groups of students. All statistical measures showed that the assessors ranked the SAL students as more competent (Millar et al., 1996; Springer et al., 1997a). As a result of this assessment, educators who had previously expressed skepticism about the effectiveness of the new approach became more open to new teaching methods.

As Garnett et al. (1995) have observed, when passive transmission of information is replaced by active learning activities, "the student is required to think carefully about the information, analyze it, and then apply it to new situations that may not have a clear solution or at first glance seem to be unrelated to the original presentation context." As a result, these researchers find that student understanding improves—*provided* the tools used to measure it are consistent with what one defines as "understanding."

As the SAL example illustrates, faculty members have considerable control over the assessment strategies they use in their own classes. These faculty members will need to consider how to improve the alignment between instructional goals and assessment tools. Tests often drive student behavior, especially at the classroom level. Researchers, teachers, and testing specialists therefore are exploring and experimenting with new assessment approaches, including discovering those that map more directly onto integrative and constructed learning. Whatever approach is chosen, assessment must at least provide feedback to teachers and students to make a fair judgment of progress and sensible next steps.

Before describing good assessment practices in current use and suggesting ways to use information technology to improve the process, it is important to define the various forms of assessment and distinguish between assessment and evaluation. The American Association for Higher Education (AAHE) defines assessment as "an ongoing process aimed at understanding and improving student learning."[15] Most definitions of evaluation, on the other hand, put little emphasis on feedback and instead concentrate on discrete measures of the overall success or failure of a process or project. Assessment often has been categorized as formative or summative. Formative assessments provide feedback to the student and instructor in a regular and systematic way, but often are not part of the student's final grade. Summative assessments measure student knowledge at the conclusion of instruction (whether a chapter, a part of a semester, or at the end of the semester), but those results are rarely used to improve teaching and learning. Although tests of various sorts are by far the most common form of assessment, other assessments that measure student ability to carry out a task (performance assessments) or the ability to apply learning to

---

[15]Available: http://www.aahe.org/assessment/ assess_faq.htm#define. [7/27/01].

the solution of real-world problems (authentic assessments) are becoming more popular.

Principles of Good Practice in Assessing Student Learning

Several national efforts are aimed at helping postsecondary faculty members reconsider assessment issues. One of these, the Assessment Forum of the AAHE, builds on the foundation laid more than a decade ago by Chickering and Gamson (1987). Although not aimed specifically at SME&T educators, the following recommendations by AAHE (1992) are flexible and relevant enough to encompass a wide range of educational innovations and can frame design assessments of information technology-based innovations in the SME&T curriculum:[16]

1. The assessment of student learning begins with educational values.
2. Assessment is most effective when it reflects an understanding of learning as multidimensional and integrated, and is revealed in performance over time.
3. Assessment works best when the programs it seeks to improve have clear, explicitly stated purposes.
4. Assessment requires attention to outcomes but also and equally to the experiences that lead to those outcomes.
5. Assessment works best when it is ongoing and not episodic.

6. Assessment fosters wider improvement when representatives from across the educational community are involved.
7. Assessment makes a difference when it begins with issues of use and illuminates questions people really care about.
8. Assessment is most likely to lead to improvement when it is part of a larger set of conditions that promote change.
9. Through assessment, educators meet responsibilities to students and to the public.

In the current climate of accountability in all types of higher education institutions, assessment must be included as a regular feature of all information technology activities. Student performance and progress will be key indicators for the next decade (Baker, 1998). Some of these assessment metrics can be as simple as usage and time on task. Others can be more probing by delving into the subtler aspects of individual or group learning. The acquisition and dissemination of data from these assessments may begin to bridge the gap between educational theory and practice. Assessment data can also help researchers and educators explore varying hypotheses about effective teaching and learning outcomes.

Using Information Technology to Assess Student Learning

While information technology is increasingly used to improve undergraduate teaching and learning, its use in assessment

---

[16]Available: http://www.aahe.org/. [7/27/01].

is lagging. Helgeson and Kumar (1993) reported that the most common use of computer technology in assessment was to administer multiple-choice tests. More recently, of the 42 university presentations at an undergraduate program directors meeting of the Howard Hughes Medical Institute (HHMI), only one mentioned using information technology in student assessment, and that involved delivering a series of multiple-choice items (HHMI, 1996). This lack of use in assessment reflects the immaturity of information technology's integration into the wider educational arena. It also underscores the fact that evaluation strategies must parallel new classroom practice and learning goals (Linn, Baker, and Dunbar, 1991) and not be neglected as information technology enables a paradigmatic shift in postsecondary teaching and learning.

Information technology offers cost and scale benefits, decreased reporting time, and increased validity in assessment of postsecondary student learning. Information technology also has the potential to:

- provide continual rather than discrete measures of student learning;
- guide assessments of student learning in complex, real-world activities;
- increase the quality of assessment data while reducing costs; and
- provide measures of learning and skills among students with special needs.

Formative Assessment Using Classroom Communication Systems

Electronic classrooms can now make formative assessment feasible even in large lecture courses where the instructor may not know students by name. Classrooms equipped with communications systems such as Classtalk[17] (see Box A-9) allow instructors to assess student understanding at crucial points during the class period, thus encouraging learning that is consistent with the research presented in this section. Traditional lectures are best suited for those students who make sense of ideas while listening and taking notes. Relying on a single instructional strategy that helps only a portion of students to learn creates inequities for all students, particularly those who assimilate materials better by discussing it, writing about it, and using it to solve problems (Dufresne, Gerace, Leonard, Mestre, and Werk, 1996).

When students discuss their answers in groups before responding to a query, their collective understanding is an example of distributed cognition. By using information technology to promote active engagement, e.g., by allowing students to run a simulation or visualize some phenomenon prior to engaging in discussions, SME&T faculty members improve the alignment between instruction and learning research.

---

[17]Available: http://www.bedu.com/. [7/27/01.]

Classtalk consists of a main computer, a set of desktop or palmtop computers or calculators, and a network that connects the two components. The instructor prepares questions beforehand, integrates them into the lecture, and poses a question either verbally or via the network. Most often, qualitative multiple-choice questions are used to check student understanding of pertinent current concepts. Students may be asked to discuss the question among themselves before responding via their computers or calculators. The instructor's computer keeps track of the responses and can display them to the whole class, if desired, in the form of a histogram or can show the instructor individual responses in the seating chart. At no time does the whole class see an individual student's response, which increases the likelihood of participation and gives the instructor a more realistic assessment of how well the class as a whole understands a particular concept. The computer provides another advantage not found in similar nontechnological approaches. Mazur (1997) was among the first to report on Classtalk, and he claims that because the computer is used to collect data on students' conceptual understanding, he has a much easier time convincing his colleagues of the validity of the data.

SOURCE: Mazur, 1997.

Digital Portfolios

Like a fine arts portfolio representing an artist's range and quality of work, a portfolio used for assessment includes samples of work that represent a student's best efforts. The portfolio could include assignments, project reports, reports on significant events, results from experiments, and reflective notes in journal format. In short, a portfolio is a collection of evidence that learning has taken place. Because portfolio assessment is designed for integration with instruction, it is becoming one of the most appealing forms of assessment, and is one area where increased use of technology in the classroom can translate directly into modified assessment activities.

Some of the benefits of portfolio assessment include:

1. By showing what they can do through their portfolios, students demonstrate skills and competencies for teachers, parents, potential employers, and even policy makers.

2. Portfolios provide useful information to evaluate comprehensively the quality of education and the quality of student achievement.

3. Because portfolios offer students a variety of ways to demonstrate what they know and can do, students are steered towards becoming reflective learners responsible for their own growth, thus encouraging and supporting multiple learning styles.

4. Portfolios offer educators multiple avenues to understand what and how their students are learning, thus contributing to

faculty efforts to design appropriate instruction that can improve student achievement.

Digital portfolios are an example of an incremental enhancement to an existing assessment based on information technology. The types of materials that might be included in a digital portfolio range from student-teacher e-mails to more complex materials such as graphics or presentations created with multimedia software tools. (See, for example, Box A-10.) Opportunities for improving assessment using digital tools depend primarily on the creativity and ingenuity of faculty and the institutional support and rewards that administrators put in place to encourage using these kinds of assessment tools.

Portfolios can require substantial effort on the part of students to produce and on the part of teachers to evaluate. Because of the new spectrum of skills displayed by students in portfolios, new rubrics to evaluate them also are needed (Gearhart, Novak, and Herman, 1996).

Assessing Problem Solving with Information Technology

Computer-based tools can be cost-effective in assessing students' problem-solving skills. For example, the Interactive Multimedia Exercises (IMMEX) Project at the University of California at Los Angeles School of Medicine,[18] which was created to

---

[18] Available: http://www.coled.umn.edu/edutech/immex/. [8/8/01].

BOX A-10 Digital Portfolio Assessment at Valley City State University

Valley City State University (Valley City, North Dakota) obtained a $1.7 million Title III grant to provide instructional technology training and equipment for its faculty and students. By the year 2000, all students who graduate will have prepared a digital portfolio that documents their best college work. This is possible in part because all full-time students are issued a laptop computer for their personal use. Students use CD-ROM-based portfolios to demonstrate their competence levels in a set of eight abilities that focus on the students' capacity to use the knowledge gained in the classroom:

Communications
Problem solving and decision making
Collaboration
Technology employment
Effective citizenship
Aesthetic responsiveness
Global perspectives
Wellness

The graphic capabilities of the CD-ROM technology enhance students' capacity to record progress and experiences.

---

assess medical students' ability to diagnose a wide variety of illnesses, has evolved into a problem-solving platform for students from elementary school onwards. IMMEX is a software package with three components:

1. An authoring tool that instructors use to design customized problems in their particular discipline;

2. A user interface for students, who are given a problem and a menu of choices for accessing information needed to solve the problem; and

3. An analysis tool that records each student's problem-solving actions in sequence.

As an assessment instrument, the most important component of IMMEX is the analysis tool, which contains embedded artificial neural networks that are "trained" to recognize problem-solving patterns. Stevens, Lopo, and Wang (1996) used this component of IMMEX to assess the ability of hundreds of UCLA medical students to correctly diagnose infectious diseases. As the first step in this process, infectious disease specialists completed six computer-based clinical diagnosis simulations. Next, the IMMEX analysis tools analyzed the diagnostic strategies used by these experts, and identified common features of their solutions to a problem. Then, these expert-trained neural networks were used to assess the diagnostic abilities of medical students. Only 17 percent of the medical students were classified as demonstrating the same strategies as the experts.

This IMMEX assessment has informed medical school faculty about areas for improvement in their efforts to train students to become capable diagnosticians. Information technology has become central to the medical school's ability to perform learning assessments of individual students that otherwise would be time- and cost-prohibitive.

CONCLUSION

The examples of curricular innovations based on information technology described in this section are by no means exhaustive. Nevertheless, they illustrate the range of ways that individuals, departments, institutions, and consortia have used information technology to give their students new, more diverse, and more authentic learning experiences. These innovations also are consistent with recommendations made in SME&T reform documents that encourage the following pedagogical and learning strategies:

- visualization
- simulation
- real-world problem solving
- collaboration
- inquiry
- design.

The projects also are consistent with what research has shown about how students learn. Finally, many of these information technology-based innovations include appropriate ongoing assessment and evaluation. They are the result of careful, deliberate planning and adequate support, features that characterize successful, sustainable reform efforts.

The next section provides an overview

of current research on teaching and learning, using examples from this section to illustrate how educational research findings can be applied in the classroom.

LEARNING USING INFORMATION TECHNOLOGY

INTRODUCTION

The committee's fundamental premise is that information technology (IT) can become a tool to enhance undergraduate science, mathematics, engineering, and technology (SME&T) learning for all students. To achieve this objective, pedagogy that includes information technology should draw on models of cognition that recognize the learning needs of today's student population.

This section of the report describes the committee's survey of recent educational research and theories. It also examines possibilities for using IT to apply these theories in undergraduate SME&T classrooms. Based on the examination discussed below, the committee found that IT can be an important vehicle to engage students and help them develop a deeper understanding of complex scientific and technical concepts.

EDUCATIONAL RESEARCH AND CURRICULUM REFORM

Traditional postsecondary instruction has relied primarily on oral presentation of fundamental science and engineering concepts, sometimes accompanied by a laboratory component for students to verify the basic principles presented during lectures. These mostly passive learning environments can help some postsecondary students learn effectively. However, the growing need for a more scientifically literate (National Research Council [NRC], 1999b) and more technologically fluent (NRC, 1999a) citizenry, combined with the increasingly multicultural backgrounds of the postsecondary student population, call those traditional methods into question. Current students, including those interested in becoming future scientists, mathematicians, and engineers, are reporting their dissatisfaction with teaching methods and course structure as well as obvious mismatches between their goals and those of the instructor (e.g., Tobias, 1990; Seymour and Hewitt, 1997).

To face this issue directly, and fueled in part by advances in neuroscience and learning theory, educational researchers have developed a deeper understanding of how people learn at different ages and have documented the importance of active engagement in the learning process (Millar et al., 1996; Springer et al., 1997a; NRC, 1999b). Fischer (1996) summarizes five fundamental assumptions about learning (p. 125):

- Learning is a process of knowledge construction, not of knowledge recording or absorption.
- Learning is knowledge-dependent; people use their existing knowledge to construct new knowledge.
- Learning is highly tuned to the situation in which it takes place.
- Learning needs to account for distributed cognition, requiring knowledge in the head of the individual learner to be combined with knowledge of the world.
- Learning is affected as much by motivational issues as by cognitive issues.

The implications of these educational research findings for postsecondary SME&T educators are becoming more widely understood and, consequently, are fueling reform initiatives. Many of the curriculum initiatives stemming from the reform movement, including those that make extensive use of information technology, have drawn on research in cognitive and social psychology, science and mathematics education, and ethnography and anthropology. This literature has stressed that students come into courses with definite beliefs and preconceptions about how the world works and that their conceptual development may involve a process of resistance, compromise, and then assimilation of new or competing knowledge.

Instructional activities also build on existing knowledge about the:

- context of learning (situated cognition);
- acquisition of knowledge across a group of individuals (distributed cognition); and
- influences of gender, ethnic and cultural influences; learning style; and motivation on student learning.

There have been significant advances in understanding the process of knowledge acquisition in the last two decades. Learning improves when instruction is contextualized (Brown, Collins, and Duguid, 1989); when it is driven by student interests and prior experiences (Shymansky et al., 1997); and when a variety of pedagogical methods are used to reach students with a diversity of learning styles (Felder, 1993).

As faculty members shift their pedagogy to the kind of instruction that is grounded in cognitive theories of learning, information technology can be a powerful instrument to help achieve these ends. As information technology plays a larger role in and out of the classroom, it will provide both structured and unstructured learning experiences. Instructors can incorporate more student-student collaboration and problem-solving activities into their courses to meet the educational needs of a diverse student population. Educators also can use information technology to assess student learning and use this information to improve teaching and learning.

LEARNING THEORIES AND EDUCATIONAL TOOLS

A variety of learning theories have been proposed based upon a large body of educational research. However, three theories of learning are particularly relevant to learning in the natural sciences: constructivism, situated cognition, and distributed cognition.

Constructivism is a model of learning that asserts that knowledge is not passively received but is actively created inside the mind of every learner.

Situated cognition contends that knowledge and skills are best acquired in contexts from daily life (Brown et al., 1989). For example, Wilson, Teslow, and Osman-Jouchoux (1995) argue that because knowledge and learning are dependent on context, the content of knowledge within a population of learners is uneven.

The central theory of distributed cognition contends that learning is distributed in an environment and among learners and is not the product of isolated individual cognitive activity (Jonassen, Campbell, and Davidson, 1994). Therefore, learners construct understanding by using a variety of resources, including other people.

Other factors not accounted for in these theories also can affect the way individuals learn. *Gender*, for example, can affect learning by shaping preferences for information presentation and processing. The research literature contains numerous well-documented studies of differences in learning

styles of male and female students. Similarly, individual differences in *motivation* to learn and achieve can profoundly impact student learning and need to be considered in developing technology-enhanced curricula. These factors, as well as the three educational theories of constructivism, situated cognition, and distributed cognition, are discussed below.

Constructivism

Theoretical Background

According to the theory of constructivism, learning is a dynamic process in which an individual actively integrates new information with existing knowledge. This idea has its roots in Jean Piaget's groundbreaking research on cognitive development in children (Herron, 1978). Piaget was the first to propose that learning has two essential components. First, learners must take in information and compare it with the information already stored in their brain, a process known as assimilation. Second, when the new information is foreign or when it is at odds with what is already known, the learner must create a new mental representation in a process called accommodation. Cognitive growth occurs when new mental representations are created or modified to fit the demands of reality. Extensions of Piaget's work have provided more precise definitions of these mental representations, or schema. Anderson (1980) describes schemas as "large, complex units of knowledge that organize much of what we know about general categories of objects, classes of events, and types of people."

According to proponents of constructivism, meaningful learning requires deliberate, personal restructuring of one's conceptual framework. Cognitive scientists have elaborated on Piaget's theories by developing several learning models. One model, proposed by Shymansky et al. (1997), proposes that learning consists of six phases (Box A-11). Three essential phases precede what Piaget referred to as the assimilation phase. During conceptual equilibrium, learners are comfortable with their present understanding. They then have an experience with a new body of information that challenges their conceptual understanding and leads to disequilibrium. Assimilation then occurs when learners adopt the new information to reestablish equilibrium. Development of new schema in accommodation is then followed by re-equilibration, a stage that persists until the next

challenge to the learners' existing knowledge structures.

Through these six phases, learners must integrate new information with prior knowledge to build more elaborate knowledge structures or schema. The role of the learner's prior experiences in developing conceptual understanding has been well documented (Bodner, 1991). Furthermore, research indicates that highly persistent misconceptions can arise from erroneous original learning, which forms a portion of the foundation of subsequent information that the student perceives as related to the existing knowledge (Zoller, 1996). Learners often retain erroneous models and explanations because they seem more reasonable and more useful to the learner (Mayer, 1987). In many cases, if not challenged, these beliefs can persist, potentially hindering further learning (McDermott, 1991; Nakhleh, 1992).

Once learners discard their misconceptions, they must then integrate their new knowledge with what Wittrock (1974) calls "generative processing." Although faculty members often "tell" students things, such as factual information in a large lecture setting, the students must become personally engaged with the material and perform mental operations on this new knowledge before the knowledge becomes their own. Robust learning best occurs when the student can examine and test the information received (Bellamy and McNeill, 1994; Wang, 1996). SME&T faculty members can select information technology-based instructional strategies to help their stu-

---

BOX A-11 The Six Phases of Learning

- conceptual equilibration
- experience
- disequilibrium
- assimilation
- accommodation
- re-equilibration

SOURCE: Shymansky et al., 1997.

dents interpret new information, reason from what is known, and solve complex problems.

Constructivism and Information Technology-Based Teaching and Learning

Models for instructional design, teaching, and learning need to reflect the ways scientists, mathematicians, and engineers create new knowledge. Likewise, these models must be grounded in current knowledge about how students learn as well as the context in which that learning takes place. In the decades since Atkin and Karplus (1962) first proposed the concept of a learning cycle, a variety of instructional models have become available to link teaching decisions with learning research (National Center for Improving Science Education, 1991). Bybee (1997) proposed one such model, known as the "5 Es" model, which contains the following elements (pp. 178-179):

1. Engage students in a learning task.
2. Enable students to explore their ideas.
3. Guide students to devise an Explanation for the observations and results of their exploration.
4. Elaborate on students' experiences by extending or applying the learning to new situations.
5. Evaluate students' explanations and understanding.

The 5 Es model can guide faculty in selecting instructional strategies that help learners overcome their misconceptions. When the learning task includes discrepant events that yield unexpected results, learners will try to understand their observations. Their exploration will naturally lead to proposals for explanations, some of which are now no longer plausible or feasible in light of the unexpected results. By letting students apply what they have learned to new situations, the instructor can help the students reinforce new conceptual understandings and permanently discard old, incorrect ones.

Many of the examples of undergraduate SME&T reform initiatives described in the previous section are grounded in educational research about student learning. For example, the use of the computer as a data-collection device is consistent with constructivist learning theory. Three programs (Studio Physics, Workshop Physics, and the Center for Science and Mathematics Teaching) extensively use Microcomputer-Based Laboratory (MBL) sensors and software. Students in these programs use the MBL tools to measure and graph such physical quantities as position, velocity, acceleration, force, temperature, light intensity, pH, pressure, sound pressure, radiation, current, and voltage. They use the results to construct their own understanding of physical phenomena in a process that mirrors the 5 Es instructional model. Students receive a scenario, discuss the scenario with other group members, suggest predictions about the outcome, and then use real-time measurement tools to collect preliminary data.

Unexpected results occur frequently, which lead the group to more rigorous experimental procedures as members struggle to make sense of an outcome that seems counterintuitive. Extensive investigation of this type of student learning demonstrates that instruction employing information technology can provide students with a conceptual understanding that is superior to other modes of instruction (Laws, 1991).

Construction of dynamic computer models is another means of implementing the 5 Es instructional paradigm. Such models encourage students to analyze, synthesize, reason, and explain complex systems (Spitulnik and Krajcik, 1998). Using information technology this way also introduces students to scientists' uses of models, as advocated by national science education reform efforts (e.g., American Association for the Advancement of Science, 1993). Casti (1997) explains why scientists use models:

- to predict a system's behavior in the future, based on the system's properties and current behavior (a predictive model);
- to provide a framework for understanding past observations as part of an overall process (an explanatory model); and
- to offer a picture of the real world with additional features built in, to let users bend or shape that reality to their own liking (a prescriptive model).

Each type of model enables learners to understand the connections between real-world concepts by constructing an environment to formulate and test a phenomenon (Spitulnik and Krajcik, 1998).

Situated Cognition

Theoretical Background

According to constructivism, learners use prior experiences and existing schema to understand new information and create new knowledge. The theory of situated cognition expands that premise by examining the context and culture in which knowledge is constructed. A central tenet of situated cognition is that learning is affected by the environment (Brown et al., 1989; Carr, Jonassen, and Litzinger, 1998; Jonassen et al., 1994). For example, some Brazilian school-age children assist their street-vendor parents by performing mathematical calculations to determine the total of a customer's purchase, despite their limited formal education (Carraher, Carraher, and Schliemann, 1985). The context of street vending contributes to developing mathematical skills.

Researchers once viewed the process of acquiring knowledge and the context in which it is applied as two separate entities. Proponents of situated cognition challenge this premise and assert that the environment should reflect how the knowledge is used (Brown et al., 1989), so that acquiring and applying knowledge becomes a cohesive, integrated process (Brown et al., 1989; Jonassen et al., 1994). Information acquired apart from its context is unusable or "inert" (Griffin and Griffin, 1996; Jonassen et al.,

1994; Young, 1993). In the aforementioned example, the marketplace gives meaning to the mathematical calculations performed by Brazilian children.

Proponents of situated cognition often use the term "cognitive apprenticeships" to describe experiences in which learners engage in "authentic practices" through activities or social interactions. The term is reminiscent of a craft apprentice who learns from a more experienced tradesperson (Brown et al., 1989; Wilson, 1993). Ultimately, the goal of cognitive apprenticeships is to promote learning in the context of an activity, culture, or tool—to allow learners to become "enculturated in a community of practice" by observing and experiencing the values and practices of a professional working community (Carr et al., 1998, p. 6). The concept of cognitive apprenticeships supports the idea that individuals must experience the culture and context for meaningful learning to occur (Wilson, 1993), which in fact happens in most graduate research in SME&T disciplines. Unlike traditional lecture instruction, cognitive apprenticeships encourage learners to develop knowledge through the modeling, coaching, and guidance of mentors (Wilson, 1993). Moreover, cognitive apprenticeships enable learners to collaborate with practitioners and gain access to the wisdom of mentors. In joining a community of practice, learners also develop their own identity as members of the community (Lave and Wenger, 1991).

Not all educators fully subscribe to situated cognition as a theory of learning. For instance, Tripp (1993) acknowledges that teaching concepts without context is an exercise in futility, but he questions the emphasis placed on immersing students in a "community of practice" without the support of classroom experience. Without a balance of authentic and classroom experiences, Tripp argues, students may gain only partially developed skills for a setting or activity. Anderson, Reder, and Simon, (1996) advocate balance when applying the principles of situated cognition, asserting that learning is both context dependent and context independent. They maintain that, while some skills develop best within the appropriate social context, other skills may be developed better via abstract instruction in classroom settings. Overall, researchers who are cautious about situated learning are not opponents of the theory *per se* but are interested in a feasible balance between practical and instructional experiences.

Situated Cognition and Information Technology-Based SME&T Learning

The examples of successful information technology-based innovations in postsecondary SME&T education described in the previous section of this appendix are consistent with research into effective, efficient learning, especially for students who historically have been underrepresented in the SME&T disciplines. Many of the examples cited are grounded in realistic, practical problems in science and engineering. These kinds of problems not only can help students integrate new information into their existing knowledge base but also can enhance their motivation to learn by providing a relevant context. The committee's examples of information technology-based courses include several instances of students working with real data on real problems of interest to professional scientists.

Distributed Cognition

Theoretical Background

Psychology has identified *cognition* as occurring "inside the head" of individuals, with only secondary influences from social, cultural, and historical factors. In effect, thought processing takes place in isolation from the context of the thought. According to Salomon (1993), such a perspective is appropriate for examining information-processing models but does not necessarily represent daily situations involving collaboration with others and the use of available tools and resources.

In contrast, the theory of *distributed cognition* holds that cognition is distributed across people, environments, situations, and objects, all of which are referred to as artifacts. Artifacts serve as vehicles that represent or act on information (Hunt, 1992; Pea, 1993). In essence, artifacts alter how a person performs a task and may compel the individual to employ entirely different cognitive skills to complete the task (Norman, 1991).

While many researchers use the term "distributed cognition," Pea refers to the same concept as "distributed intelligence" to make the distinction that "people, not designed objects, 'do' cognition" (Pea, 1993, p. 50). For the discussion that follows, "distributed cognition" and "distributed intelligence" are used interchangeably.

In his study of distributed cognition among airline crew members, Norman (1992) identified numerous instances where crew members used common objects as artifacts to communicate information. This study was motivated by a tragic circumstance. A plane crashed—reportedly, because the captain had a heart attack that went undetected by the first officer, who dismissed the captain's unresponsive behavior as typical and, therefore, not alarming. This example illustrates several principles of distributed cognition, including the danger of having all the knowledge reside in one individual (Norman, 1992). As with so many activities, a commercial plane cannot be flown by a single individual but requires collaboration among all crew members. Distributed cognition also discourages cognitive overload, in which individuals either fail to notice critical pieces of information or concentrate on a single explanation to the exclusion of other possibilities.

Distributed Cognition and SME&T Learning

Group learning, in which students draw on and learn from the experiences of others, is one manifestation of distributed cognition. Collaborative learning and cooperative learning are two forms of group learning. Although similar, the concepts are not synonymous. Collaborative learning is "…an umbrella term for a variety of educational approaches involving joint intellectual effort by students, or by students and teachers together" (Goodsell et al., 1990). Cooperative learning (Box A-12), a form of collaborative learning, is an instructional technique that allows students to work in groups to achieve a common goal, to which they each contribute in individually accountable ways (Slavin, 1995). Learning increases when students learn interactively in groups (Brufee, 1993). For example, in a meta-analysis of published research on undergraduate SME&T education, Springer et al. (1997b) found that small-group learning results in greater academic achievement, better attitudes toward learning, and increased persistence in SME&T courses. Johnson, Johnson, and Smith (1998) conducted a similar meta-analysis and came to the same conclusion—namely, that cooperative learning promotes higher individual achievement than either competitive or individualistic approaches to learning. These findings seem to hold regardless of discipline or class size. Group learning in biology (Watson and Marshall, 1995), chemistry (Wright, 1996), earth science (Macdonald and Korinek, 1995), and physics (Hake, 1998) all resulted in greater student achievement than did courses where students worked independently.

The committee reviewed several examples of curricula that incorporate collaborative learning techniques. The Workshop

> ## BOX A-12 Key Elements of Cooperative Learning
>
> - Students understand that their success depends on the success of others in their group.
> - Activities and assessments are structured to allow for individual accountability.
> - Students are expected to promote one another's success.
> - Faculty members teach students the social skills needed for cooperative endeavors.
> - Students are encouraged to reflect on the group's learning process.
>
> SOURCE: Johnson et al., 1998.

Physics curriculum[19] uses cooperative learning strategies for guided inquiry activities and student projects. Likewise, students using BioQuest curriculum materials[20] work in groups. The University of California at Los Angeles' Science Challenge[21] offers lower-division students hands-on experience using real scientific problems, and provides support structures that foster teamwork rather than pitting students against

---

[19] Available: http://physics.dickinson.edu/ PhysicsPages/Workshop_Physics/Workshop_Physics_ Home.htm. [7/27/01].

[20] Available: http://bioquest.org. [7/27/01.]

[21] Available: http://www.nslc.ucla.edu/SciChal. html. [7/27/01].

their peers. These and other information technology-based curriculum innovations use a distributed-cognition learning model. Group members are responsible for gathering data on a facet of a problem, sharing that data and their knowledge with other group members, and integrating that knowledge into the overall solution to the problem.

The examples identified also enable students to connect to rich resources on a network and communicate with their peers outside the classroom, consistent with the precepts of distributed cognition and, to some degree, situated cognition. Class activities that incorporate distributed intelligence encourage students to assume greater ownership and participation in learning. Students actually become "inventors of distributed-intelligence-as-tool, rather than receivers of intelligence-as-substance" (Pea, 1993, p. 82). Information technology affords students the resources to tackle their assignments more fully by accessing databases, the Internet, and other materials. And the mark of a successful student is generally the one who accesses a variety of diverse resources and then uses the information inventively to solve problems and complete tasks (Fischer, 1996; Pea, 1993). In the BioQuest instructional modules, complex simulations of real phenomena are used to generate data for student problem solving. The processes students use to solve a problem, including the resources they access, also provide the instructor with a great deal of insight about student understanding of the problem. In Project Interac-

tive Multimedia Exercises, SME&T educators can use information technology to track student analytical skills by documenting each step in problem solving, which is virtually impossible to do with any other method. Harley (1993) points out that in situated learning settings such as this, the instructor's role becomes supportive rather than directive. Such a role can be equally demanding, since the instructor must determine which problems to explore, provide the necessary background learning or "scaffolding," and assess and reassess the situated learning that occurs (Young, 1993).

Distance learning courses also illustrate the application of distributed cognition. For example, Professor Kawagley's "Native Ways of Knowing" at the University of Alaska enable students who are separated both physically and culturally to engage in cooperative learning (see Box A-13). The emphasis in the Alaska example is not on the thought process and work of individuals *per se* but more on how group members exchange thoughts and ideas to complete the assignment. This project exemplifies the essence of distributed cognition, in which thought processing occurs between group members and by means of a diverse set of resources.

Gender Differences in the Learning Process

Theoretical Background

An article in *The Washington Post*, headlined "Gender Gap in Fairfax Computer

At the University of Alaska, Professor Angayuqaq Kawagley offers a cross-listed Native Studies/Education course that addresses the ways that Native Alaskan cultures use empirical knowledge to derive abstract knowledge about the natural world and link this with modern scientific knowledge. Using compressed-video technology and electronic mail, 36 students of various ethnic groups from communities separated by hundreds of miles participate in the course. Class "meetings" are broadcast live over television throughout rural Alaska, creating an unexpectedly large unenrolled audience.

The technology allowed students to remain in their physical and cultural context during the course. Instead of the usual difficulties that diverse learners face in relating course content to their personal circumstances, contextual interpretation was explicitly discussed. Discussion of context added a critical dimension to learning about science. Together, students realized that single perspectives or explanations of natural phenomena are incomplete; accepting all explanations simultaneously is incoherent. Pressed to consider the logic internal to their own culture, each student also could press for the same coherence from other cultures.

[1]Available: http://www.ankn.uaf.edu/nwkt.html. [7/27/01].

Classes," reported on the disproportionate number of male students who take high school computer classes in the Fairfax County, Virginia, school system when compared with the number of female students enrolled.[22] The 3-to-1 ratio of males to females in these classes is part of a national trend, according to a report by the American Association of University Women (AAUW, 1998). AAUW convened the AAUW Educational Foundation Commission to Examine Gender, Technology, and Teacher Education in order to study the underlying causes of gender difference in computer usage.[23] Do males and females use computers differently? Do teachers contribute to gender-related differences in students' attitudes toward computers and learning with or about computers? What can be attributed to the fact that computers and user interfaces were mainly developed by males (NRC, 1997a)? Are males more predisposed than females to exhibit strength in visual-spatial skills, which computer-based learning emphasizes? Regardless of the eventual outcome, studying these differences will contribute to understanding and possibly correcting any inequities in access to high-technology.

Research to understand gender differences in learning has increased during the

[22]Benning, V. 1998. Gender Gap in Fairfax Computer Classes: Report Says Boys Outnumber Girls 3 to 1; Some Minorities Also Underrepresented. *Washington Post.* July 14:B1, B5.

[23]Available: http://www.aauw.org/2000/. [7/27/01].

last 20 years and has included studies of a variety of age groups. These studies have ranged from examinations of verbal abilities to studies of visual-spatial skills in females and males. The finding that males consistently score higher than females on science tests (Howe and Dowdy, 1989) suggests the need for further research on gender differences. Hamilton (1995) suggests several explanations for different SME&T achievement between males and females. Although environmental factors and personal experiences can influence a student's ability to learn and apply information, biological and physiological factors also can affect that learning, although to what extent remains under debate (NRC, 1999b).

Neuroscientists who study gender differences in learning have focused their investigations on the anatomy and physiology of the brain, particularly the lateralization (specialization) of the brain's two hemispheres to perform specific tasks. Language, for example, is thought to reside primarily in the left hemisphere, while visual-spatial processing occurs predominantly in the right hemisphere. However, some researchers have hypothesized that females have better verbal abilities because language resides in both hemispheres of the brain in women but is primarily lateralized in the left hemisphere in men. By using magnetic resonance imaging to track brain activity during language tasks, Shaywitz et al. (1995) demonstrated that these tasks primarily involved the left brain hemisphere among males, while, among women, the same region of both hemispheres was active. These

results are consistent with the current hypothesis about hemispheric specialization, but Shaywitz et al. (1995) also acknowledge that other regions in the brain may contribute to phonological and language tasks. If, in fact, language is bilateralized across both hemispheres of the brain in females, then the theory of "cognitive crowding" proposed by Levy (1976) becomes more plausible. Levy argued that visual-spatial cognition, which is typically attributed to the right hemisphere, must share neural space with language functioning in the right hemisphere in females. In comparison, language functioning for males is lateralized to the left hemisphere, allowing more neural space in the right hemisphere for functioning related to visual-spatial activities.

Gender Differences and Information Technology-Based Learning

Although there is an extensive body of research from many areas of science that attempts to identify underlying biological explanations for differences in cognition between males and females, many studies have simply documented these differences without attempting to attribute them to either physiological or social factors. These studies are useful because they help to identify fertile areas for research on the underlying causes of gender differences in cognition and, equally important, because they often have immediate, practical applications.

For example, Hall and Hickman (1997) conducted a study in which 27 undergraduate psychology students ranging from 19 to 45 years old evaluated five Web pages that described a neuron. Three of the pages consisted of text, one page consisted of a picture of the neuron, and one page consisted of both the text and the neuron. The background of three of the pages varied in complexity, which allowed investigators to investigate the effects of both the form of information and the context in which it was delivered. After reviewing the pages, students answered a questionnaire regarding their age, gender, experience with computers, and experience with the World Wide Web. Results indicated that both sexes gave higher ratings to the Web pages that contained both the text and the picture of the neuron; however, results also revealed a significant difference between male and female ratings regarding the visual complexity of the Web pages. The men gave a higher rating to the more visually complex pages, while women rated those pages lower on the scale. While Hall and Hickman (1997) stated that females reported less experience with computers and the World Wide Web than did men, this factor did not seem to account for the significant difference in the complexity ratings.

Learning Styles

Theoretical Background

In an era of increasing student diversity, educators can enhance learning opportunities for all students by being more aware of learning differences. It has been well estab-

lished that individuals develop a preferred, consistent set of behaviors or approaches to learning (Litzinger and Osif, 1993). This set of behaviors, otherwise known as a learning style, can be described in terms of four layers (Curry, 1983), with different learning styles tending to concentrate on one of the layers:

1. The *personality layer* describes an individual's basic personality, often in a continuum from introvert to extrovert.
2. The *information processing layer* refers to the way a learner prefers to take in and process information.
3. The *social interactions layer* centers on how students behave and interact in the classroom (e.g., focused solely on learning or on grades).
4. The *instructional preference layer* describes the mode in which learning occurs most easily (e.g., listening, reading, and direct experience).

These learning style layers are not independent of each another, since the traits of one level will influence the next. Nonetheless, cognitive psychologists have developed a number of models for each of the layers. For a comprehensive review of these models, see Claxton and Murrell (1987), who focused on how these layers overlap; options for helping students determine and understand their own learning style; trends in gender-related differences in learning style; and the implications of this information for SME&T faculty members.

Two models of learning styles have become widely accepted, in part because of simple-to-use instruments that help determine a student's learning style. Kolb's model of experiential learning (1984) describes learning as a continuum from concrete to abstract and from active to reflective. The resulting 2×2 matrix yields four learning styles, as shown in Table A-2.

Felder (1996) proposed another model of learning styles. In his model, five key questions are posed to probe a student's learning preferences:

- Does the learner prefer sensory information (sights, sounds, and physical sensations) or intuitive information (memories, ideas, and insights)?
- Does the learner perceive sensory information most effectively through visual or verbal modes?
- Does the learner prefer to process information actively or reflectively?
- How does the learner progress toward understanding, sequentially or globally?
- Is the learner more comfortable with information that is obtained inductively (principles inferred from facts and observations) or deductively (consequences and applications inferred from principles)?

Felder and Soloman[24] have developed a "Learning Styles Inventory" to help students answer the first four of Felder's questions about their own learning. Like Kolb (1984) and Curry (1983), Felder (1993, 1996) sees these traits as a continuum and describes students according to their preference for one mode or another. He further argues that, although students may be uncomfortable with instruction in their less-preferred modes of learning, faculty members should teach in multiple modes to accommodate the range of individual differences in a class (Felder, 1996). In the end, much of the responsibility for learning lies with the individual student. Knowledge about one's own learning style is only useful if students know what to do with that information. After students complete the Learning Styles Inventory, Felder provides them with a handout of tips for maximizing their learning in ways that are consistent with their own learning style.[25]

Learning Styles and SME&T Education

Information technology-based instruction has particular implications for the in-

TABLE A-2 *Kolb's Learning Styles as a Continuum from Concrete to Abstract and from Active to Reflective*

	Reflective	Active
Concrete	"Why?"	"What if?"
Abstract	"What?"	"How?"

SOURCE: Kolb, 1984.

[24]Available: http://www2.ncsu.edu/unity/lockers/users/f/felder/public/ILSdir/ILS-a.htm. [7/27/01].

[25]Available: http://www2.ncsu.edu/unity/lockers/users/f/felder/public/ILSdir/styles.htm. [7/27/01].

formation processing and instructional preference layers in Curry's model of learning styles (Curry, 1983). Information technology can help SME&T faculty members address the learning needs of all of their students by offering students instruction in a more preferred mode. Active learners, for instance, like to discuss ideas with their classmates or solve problems in a group setting. Electronic communications technologies make this possible even when students are in different locations. Information technology is especially helpful for visual learners, who gain more from pictures and diagrams than they do from the written and spoken words that fill most lecture classes. Sensory learners prefer facts and observations to concepts and interpretations and can be frustrated by courses devoid of real-world context.

Traditional lecture courses best serve students who are intuitive rather than sensory learners (Godleski, 1984). Faculty members who use information technology to provide science and mathematics instruction are likely to enhance student retention in their courses by maintaining the interest and motivation of students with other learning styles. The examples discussed in this document showcase how information technology could present information in a variety of ways. Computers offer unique information processing capabilities, such as multiple representations, interactive real-time assessment, and document revision, all of which can help individual students better construct their own understanding (Spitulnik and Krajcik, 1998). In addition,

the use of multiple representations (diagrams, drawings, graphs, animations, and video) more closely approximates the way that scientists understand and describe phenomena, and can help students understand scientific concepts (Kozma and Quellmalz, 1995). Multiple representations of information also allow faculty members greater flexibility and creativity in developing effective pedagogical practices.

Finally, the use of multiple representations can make SME&T courses more inclusive for all students, not just those who learn the same way as their instructors. Halpern (1992) emphasized that knowledge about learning styles can be used to facilitate and improve curricula and instruction for both sexes. Material in SME&T courses can be presented in multiple ways, and various aspects of problem solving can incorporate both visual-spatial and verbal skills. Information technology-based initiatives that allow students to visualize complex phenomena, such as mathematical functions or molecular structures in three dimensions, can broaden the range of learning styles the instructor can accommodate.

For example, visualization of mathematical functions is central to the use of information technology in the calculus initiatives described in the previous section. Project CLEA[26] is another program that makes use of visualization of complex phenomena to teach. It allows students to con-

---

[26]Contemporary Laboratory Experiences in Astronomy. Available: http://www.gettysburg.edu/project/physics/clea/CLEAhome.html. [7/27/01].

struct and manipulate images of stars and other astronomical bodies constructed from digital data. The Molecular Science Initiative at UCLA[27] uses molecular modeling hardware and software to provide students with images of phenomena that are otherwise impossible to visualize without information technology tools. Projects that feature GIS usage or multimedia tools similarly enable instructors to reach students with a variety of preferred learning styles.

The Role of Motivation in Learning

Theoretical Background

The role of science education is to help learners grow in all three educational domains: cognitive, psychomotor, and affective. The development of problem-solving and reasoning skills and the acquisition of facts and concepts occur in the cognitive domain, while the development of physical and dexterity skills takes place in the psychomotor domain. The affective domain incorporates the learner's motivation, attitudes, and beliefs.

The keys to success in education often are rooted in how a student feels about home, self, and school. These factors can confound efforts to transform postsecondary SME&T education because much of the affective domain is well established before students complete high school. Motivating students to learn science is perhaps the

greatest challenge for SME&T educators. Unfortunately, current teaching practices often dampen student motivation and interest in science. The information technology-based initiatives highlighted in this document have been successful in part because they are sensitive to the affective dimensions of learning. The examples showcase a variety of instructional strategies and indicate how they accommodate a wide range of learning styles.

Motivation affects the likelihood that students will persist in a course. If success is defined partly in terms of a student's course completion, student motivation becomes an important consideration.

McMillan and Forsyth (1991) define motivation as "purposeful engagement in classroom tasks and study to master concepts and skills." Although this definition may need to be broadened to encompass non-campus based learning (vis-à-vis "classroom" tasks), it nonetheless suggests important research questions about the catalysts for engagement and student persistence mastering subject matter.

As discussed above in the section on situated cognition, some motivation to learn derives from the link between the information being learned and its application. If the information seems irrelevant, students may not pay close attention to the details, and this can lead to misconceptions (Cognition and Technology Group at Vanderbilt University, 1993). While there are several ways to define "relevance," ultimately, it is in the mind of the learner. When courses and assignments incorporate the kinds of

---

[27]Available: http://www.mosci.ucla.edu. [7/30/01].

experiences described in the previous section, increased motivation and "time on task" may help students focus not only on the "big picture" but also on those very details that will help them build a solid foundation for further learning of SME&T.

Student Motivation and Information Technology-Based Education

Student interest and satisfaction with instructional materials also can enhance motivation. For example, multimedia approaches can increase student motivation and interest (Fifield and Peifer, 1994; Powers, 1998). Multimedia can be fun, and "having fun with learning may enhance motivation and achievement" (Druger, 1997). Information Technology can also be used to tailor instruction to the needs and learning styles of individual students. Instruction that recognizes how much each student has already mastered and what significant questions remain can enhance motivation and learning.

For example, physicists at the U.S. Air Force Academy, Indiana University-Purdue University Indianapolis, and Davidson College have collaborated to develop Just in Time Teaching (Novak, Patterson, and Gavrin, 1999). In this approach, instructors develop web-based assignments, and students respond electronically. The instructor reads the student submissions "just in time" to adjust the lesson content and activities to suit the students' needs. This creates a feed-back loop, in which student preparation outside of class fundamentally affects what happens during the classroom session. As a result, most students come to class already prepared and engaged with the material. And, the faculty member knows at the beginning of class exactly how much each student has learned and how to best spend the classroom time. Originally developed to support physics instruction, more than 60 colleges and universities are now using this approach to provide instruction in a variety of academic disciplines (Novak, Patterson, and Gavrin, 2001). It appears that Just in Time Teaching motivates students to increase both the amount and quality of their interactions with other students and with faculty, as well as increasing their time on educational tasks. One extensive study found that these three factors—student-student interaction, student-faculty interaction, and time on task are critical to success in the undergraduate years (Astin, 1993).

Motivation, attitudes, and beliefs are equally important for "traditional" and "nontraditional" postsecondary SME&T learners and must be considered when developing courses and curricula for nontraditional populations of students. Many researchers contend that the motivators for adult learners are quite different from those of other populations. For example, Cennamo and Dawley (1995) found that internal motivators such as self-esteem, quality of life, and increased job satisfaction are far more important to adult learners than external motivators such as grades.

CONCLUSION

There is now considerable research on how students learn science and mathematics and how best to teach these disciplines (e.g., Gabel, 1990; NRC, 1999b). This research has contributed to the growing diversity of instructional strategies in postsecondary SME&T education (McNeal and D'Avanzo, 1997; Glassick et al., 1997). This trend must continue so that greatest potential learning gains from the use of information technology for teaching and learning SME&T can be achieved.

The applications of information technology that are described in this section are firmly grounded in the educational research literature. They are based on what is known about how students learn, both individually and in groups, and about how to establish inclusive learning opportunities that student find relevant to their personal experience and goals. These applications also share another important feature: considerable effort was expended on designing, evaluating, and using the outcomes of those evaluations to improve each application. This process of continual improvement also has catalyzed further research. Each application has contributed to the growing body of literature about educational assessment methods.

REFERENCES & BIBLIOGRAPHY

Accreditation Board for Engineering and Technology. (1997). *Criteria for accrediting programs in engineering in the United States*. Baltimore, MD: Author. Available: http://www.abet.org. [7/27/01].

Alexander, P.A. and Judy, J.E. (1988). Interaction of Domain-Specific and Strategic Knowledge in Academic Performance. *Review of Educational Research*, 58(4):375-404.

American Association for Higher Education. (1992). *Principles of good practice for assessing student learning*. Washington, DC: Author.

American Association for the Advancement of Science. (1993). *Benchmarks for science literacy*. New York: Oxford University Press.

American Association of University Women. (1998). *Gender gap: Where schools still fail our children*. Washington, DC: Author.

Anderson, J R. (1980). *Cognitive psychology and its implications*. San Francisco: W.H. Freeman & Co.

Anderson, J.R. (1983). *The architecture of cognition*. Cambridge, MA: Harvard University Press.

Anderson, J.R. (1995). *Cognitive psychology and its implications*. New York: W.H. Freeman & Co.

Anderson, J.R., Reder, L.M., and Simon, H.A. (1996). Situated Learning and Education. *Education Researcher*, 4(5):5-11.

Astin, A.W. (1993). *What matters in college? Four critical years revisited*. San Francisco: Jossey-Bass.

Atkin, M.J. and Karplus, R.H. (1962). Discovery or Invention? *The Science Teacher*, 29(2):121-143.

Baker, E.L. (1998). *Model-based performance assessment*. CSE Technical Report 465. Los Angeles: University of California, National Center for Research on Evaluation, Standards, and Student Testing.

Baker, W., Hale, T., and Gifford, B.R. (1997). From Theory to Implementation: The Mediated Learning Approach to Computer-Mediated Instruction, Learning, and Assessment. *EDUCOM Review*, 32(5):42-50.

Balestri, D., Ehrmann, S.C., and Ferguson, D.L. (1992). Preface (pp. xi-xiv), *Learning to design, designing to learn: Using technology to transform the curriculum*. NY: Taylor & Francis.

Basili, P.A. and P.J. Sanford. (1991). Conceptual change strategies and cooperative group work in chemistry. *Journal of Research in Science Teaching*, 28(4):293-304.

Baxter, G.P., Elder, A.D, and Glaser, R. (1997). Assessment and Instruction in the Science Classroom. *CSE Technical Report 432*. Los Angeles: University of California, National Center for Research on Evaluation, Standards, and Student Testing.

Bellamy, L. and McNeill, B. (1994). *Active learning in the engineering classroom*. Instructional Materials for Classroom Use, College of Engineering and Applied Sciences. Tempe, AZ: Arizona State University.

Benning, V. (1998, July 14). Gender Gap in Fairfax Computer Classes: Report Says Boys Outnumber Girls 3 to 1; Some Minorities Also Underrepresented. *Washington Post*, pp. B1, B5.

Benoit, R. (1998). Mr. Chips Meets Computer Chip: the Consequences of the Microbial Literacy Project of 21st Century Teaching of General Microbiology. *Focus on Microbiology Education*, 4:1.

Berger, C. (1998). Ann Jackson and the Four Myths of Integrating Technology into Teaching. *Syllabus*, March:18-20.

Berselli, B. (1997, September 30). Read It and Weep: Online Publishing Actually Boosts Sales. *Washington Post*, pp. C1-C2.

Birk, J.P. and Foster, J. (1993). The importance of lecture in general chemistry course performance. *Journal of Chemistry Education*, 70:180-182.

Bloom B.S. and Krathwohl, D.R. (1956). *Taxonomy of educational objectives: The classification of educational goals*. New York: Longmans, Green.

Blumer, H. (1969). *Symbolic interactionism: Perspective and method*. Berkeley, CA: University of California Press.

Bodner, G.M. (1991). I Have Found You an Argument: The Conceptual Knowledge of Beginning Chemistry Graduate Students. *Journal of Chemistry Education*, 68:385-388.

Borgman, C. (Ed). (1990). *Scholarly communications and biblitometrics*. Newbury Park: Sage Publications.

Bourque, D.R. and Carlson, G.R. (1987). Hands-on Versus Computer Simulation Methods in Chemistry. *Journal of Chemistry Education*, 64:232-234.

Boverie, P., Nagel, L., and Garcia, S. (1997). Learning Styles, Emotional Intelligence, and Social Presence as Predictors of Distance Education Student Satisfaction. *Selected papers from the eighth national conference on college teaching and learning*. Jacksonville, FL: Florida Community College at Jacksonville.

Boyer Commission on Educating Undergraduates in the Research University. (1998). *Reinventing undergraduate education: A blueprint for America's research universities*. Stony Brook, NY: Author.

Brown, A.L. (1978). Knowing when, where and how to remember: A problem of metacognition. Pp. 367-406 in R. Glaser (Ed.), *Advances in instructional psychology*. Hillsdale, NJ: Erlbaum.

Brown, A.L., Bransford, J.D., Ferrara, R.A., and Campione, J.C. (1983). Learning Remembering and Understanding. In J.H. Flavell and E.M. Markman (Eds.) *Handbook of child psychology*: Vol. 3, Cognitive Development (4th ed.).

Brown, J.S., Collins, A., and Duguid, P. (1989). Situated Cognition and the Culture of Learning. *Education Researcher*, 18:32-42.

Brufee, K.A. (1993). *Collaborative learning: Higher education, interdependence, and the authority of* knowledge. Baltimore: The Johns Hopkins University Press.

Bybee, R.W. (1997). *Achieving science literacy: From purposes to practice.* Portsmouth, NH: Heinemann.

Carr, A.A., Jonassen, D.H., and Litzinger, M.E. (1998). Good Ideas to Foment Educational Revolution: The Role of Systemic Change in Advancing Situated Learning, Constructivism, and Feminist Pedagogy. *Educational Technology,* 38(1):5-15.

Carraher, T.N., Carraher, D.W., and Schliemann, A.D. (1985). Mathematics in the Streets and in Schools. *British Journal of Developmental Psychology,* 3:21-29.

Casti, J.L. (1997). *Would-be worlds: How simulation is changing the frontiers of science.* New York: J. Wiley.

Cech, T.R. (1999). Science at Liberal Arts Colleges: A Better Education? *Daedalus, 128* (1), Winter:195-216.

Cennamo, K.S. and Dawley, G.W. (1995). Designing Interactive Video Materials for Adult Learners. *Performance & Improvement,* 34(1):14-19.

Chase, W.G. and Simon, H.A. (1973). Perception in chess. *Cognitive Psychology,* 4:55-81.

Chi, M.T.H., Feltovich, P.J., and Glaser, R. (1981). Categorization and Representation of Physics Problems by Experts and Novices. *Cognitive Science,* 5:121-152.

Chickering, A.W. and Gamson, Z.E. (1987). Seven Principles for Good Practice in Undergraduate Education. *American Association for Higher Education Bulletin,* 39(7):3-7.

Choi, J.I. and Hannafin, M. (1995). Situated cognition and learning environments: Roles, Structures, and implications for design. *Educational Technology, Research, and Development,* 43(2):53-69.

Chonacky, N. and Myers, J. (1997). Exploring Collaboratory Partnerships for Interdisciplinary Undergraduate Science Education Reform. *Council on Undergraduate Research Quarterly,* 18(1):18-23.

Claxton, C.S. and Murrell, P.H. (1987). Learning Styles: Implications for Improving Educational Practices. *ASHE-ERIC Higher Education Report No. 4.* Washington, DC: George Washington University.

Clinton, W.J. (1997). Opening College Doors to All Americans: Excerpts from Remarks at San Jacinto Community College. *Journal of Chemistry Education,* 74(12):1392-1393.

Cognition and Technology Group at Vanderbilt University. (1993). Anchored Instruction and Situated Cognition Revisited. *Educational Technology,* 33(3):52-70.

Cole, M. and Engestrom, Y. (1993). A cultural-historical approach to distributed cognition. Pp. 1-46 in G. Salomon (Ed.), *Distributed cognitions: Psychological and educational considerations.* Cambridge, UK: Cambridge University Press.

Coley, R.J., Cradler, J., and Engel, P.K. (1997). *Computers and classrooms: The status of technology in U.S. schools.* Princeton, NJ: Educational Testing Service.

Collins, A. (1988). *Cognitive apprenticeship and instructional technology* (Report No. BBN-R-6899). Cambridge, MA: BBN Laboratories. (ERIC Document Reproduction Service No. ED 331 465).

Collis, B. (1997). Cooperative Learning on the World Wide Web. *Selected Papers from the Eighth National Conference on College Teaching and Learning.* Jacksonville, FL: Florida Community College at Jacksonville.

Consumer Electronics Association. (1996). *Senior market potential.* Arlington, VA: Author. Available: http://www.ebrain/org/ers/crs_all.asp. [October 24, 2001].

Crouch, R.D., Holden, M.S., and Samet, C. (1996). CAChe Molecular Modeling: A Visualization Tool Early in the Undergraduate Curriculum. *Journal of Chemistry Education,* 73(10):916-917.

Curry, L. (1983, April). An Organization of Learning Styles Theory and Constructs. Paper presented at the American Educational Research Association annual meeting, Montreal.

Daniel, J.S. (1996). *Mega-universities and knowledge media: technology strategies for higher education.* London: Kogan Page.

Davis, P. (1997). What Computer Skills do Employers Expect from Recent College Graduates? *Technological Horizons in Education,* Sept:74-78.

Department for Education and Employment (UK). (1997). *Connecting the learning society.* London: Author.

Derry, S.J., DuRussel, L.A., and O'Donnell, A.M. (1997). *Individual and distributed cognitions in interdisciplinary teamwork: A developing case study and emerging theory.* Madison, WI: National Institute for Science Education.

DiAmico, M., Baron, L.J., and Sissons, M.E. (1995). Gender Differences in Attributions about Microcomputer Learning. *Sex Roles, 33:*353-385.

Doerr, John. (1998, March 16). *Business Week,* p 29.

Druger, M. (1997). Motivating the Unmotivated. In E. Siebert, M. Caprio, and C. Lyda (Eds.), *Effective teaching and course management.* Dubuque, IA: Kendall-Hunt.

Duderstadt, J.J. (1997). The Future of the University in an Age of Knowledge. *Journal of Asynchronous Learning Networks, 1*(2):78-88.

Dufresne, R.J., Gerace, W.J., Leonard, W.J., Mestre, J.P., and Wenk, L. (1996). Classtalk: A Classroom Communication System for Active Learning in the College Lecture Hall. *Journal of Computing and Higher Education, 7:*3-47.

Dyson, E. (1997) *Release 2.0.* New York: Broadway Books, Bantam Doubleday Dell Publishing Group.

Ehrmann, S.C. (1988). Improving a Distributed Learning Environment with Computers and Telecommunications. Pp. 255-259 in R. Mason and A.Kaye (Eds.), *Mindweave: Communication,*

computers and distance education. New York: Pergamon Press.

Ehrmann, S.C. (1990). Reaching Students, Reaching Resources: Using Technologies to Open the College. *Academic Computing, IV*(7):10-14, 32-34.

Ehrmann, S.C. and Balestri, D. (1992). Learning to Design, Designing to Learn: A More Creative Role for Technology. pp. 1-20. In D. Balestri, S. Ehrmann, and D. Ferguson (Eds.), *Learning to design, designing to learn: Using technology to transform the curriculum.* New York: Taylor & Francis.

Ellis, J.D. (1990). Preparing Science Teachers for the Information Age. *Journal of Computers in Mathematics and Science Teaching, 9*(4):55-70.

Ercolano, V. (1998). Students, Start Your Designs! *American Society for Engineering Education Prism, 7*(5):16.

Esiobu, G.O. and Soyibo, K. (1995). Effects of concept and vee mapping under three learning modes on students' cognitive achievement in ecology and genetics. *Journal of Research in Science Teaching, 32*(9): 971-95.

Faison, C.L. (1996). Modeling Instructional Technology Use in Teacher Preparation: Why We Can't Wait. *Educational Technology, XXXVI*(5):47-59.

Felder, R.M. (1993). Reaching the Second Tier: Learning and Teaching Styles in College Science Education. *Journal of College Science Teaching, 22*(5):286-290.

Felder, R.M. (1996). Matters of Style. *American Society for Engineering Education Prism, 6*(4):18-23.

Fifield, S.J. and Peifer, R.W. (1994). Enhancing Lecture Presentations in Introductory Biology with Computer-Based Multimedia. *Journal of College Science Teaching, 23:*235-239.

Fischer, G. (1995). Distributed Cognition, Learning Webs, and Domain-Oriented Design Environments. Pp. 125-129 in *Proceedings of the conference on computer supported for collaborative learn-*

ing. Available: http://www-cscl95.indiana.edu/ cscl95/fischer.html. [7/27/01].

Fischer, G. (1996, June). Making Learning a Part of Life: Beyond the Gift Wrapping Approach to Technology. Paper presented at the National Science Foundation Symposium, Learning and Intelligent Systems. Available: http:// www.cs.colorado.edu/~l3d/presentations/gf-wlf/. [7/27/01].

Flavell, J.H. (1979). Metacognition and Cognitive Monitoring: A New Era of Cognitive-Development Inquiry. *American Psychologist, 34*:906-911.

Floyd, B.P. (1998, September 11). Professor's Web Site Makes Her "Dear Abby of Math." *Chronicle of Higher Education*, p. A31.

Gabel, D.L. (1990). Students' Understanding of the Particle Nature of Matter and its Relationship to Problem-Solving. Pp. 92-105 in *Empirical research in mathematics and science education.* Proceedings of the International Seminar, University of Dortmund, Germany.

Garmer, A.K. and Firestone, C.M. (1996). *Creating a learning society: Initiatives for technology and education.* Washington, DC: The Aspen Institute.

Garnett, P.J., Hacking, M., and Oliver, R. (1995). Refocusing the Chemistry Lab: A Case for Laboratory-Based Investigations. *Australian Science Teachers Journal, 41*(2):26-32.

The Gartner Group, Inc. (1993). *Management strategies: PC cost/benefit and payback analysis.* Stamford, CT: Author.

Gearhart, M., Novak, J.R., and Herman, J.L. (1996). Issues in Portfolio Assessment: The Scorability of Narrative Collections. *CSE Tech. Report No. 410.* Los Angeles: University of California, National Center for Research on Evaluation, Standards, and Student Testing.

Gick, M.L. and McGarry, S.J. (1992). Learning From Mistakes: Inducing Analogous Solution Failures to a Source Problem Produces Later Successes in Analogical Transfer. *Journal of*

Experimental Psychology: Learning, Memory and Cognition, 18:623-639.

Gilbert, S.W. (1996). Posted to the American Association for Higher Education information technology listserve (aahesgit@list.cren.net), 1/ 23/96. Subject: AAHESGIT: 10th of 14; Support Service Crisis.

Glanz, J. (1998). Cosmos in a Computer. *Science, 280*:1522-1523.

Glaser, R. (1991). Expertise and assessment. Pp. 17-30 in M.C. Wittrock and E.L. Baker (Eds.), *Testing and cognition.* Englewood Cliffs, NJ: Prentice Hall.

Glassick, C.E., Huber, M.T., and Maeroff, G. I. (1997). *Scholarship assessed: Evaluation of the professoriate.* San Francisco: Jossey-Bass.

Glennan, T.K. and Melmed, A. (1996). *Fostering the use of educational technology: Elements of a national strategy.* Santa Monica, CA: Rand.

Gobbo, C., and Chi, M.T.H. (1986). How knowledge is structured and used by expert and novice children. *Cognitive Development, 1*:221-237.

Godleski, E. (1984). Learning Style Compatibility of Engineering Students and Faculty. Proceedings, Annual Frontiers in Education Conference. American Society for Engineering Education/ Institute of Electronic and Electrical Engineers, Philadelphia, PA.

Goodsell, A., Maher, M., Tinto, V., Smith, B.L., and MacGregor, J., (Eds.) (1990). *Collaborative learning: A sourcebook for higher education.* University Park, PA: National Center on Postsecondary Teaching, Learning, and Assessment.

Graves, W.H. (1997). A Framework for Universal Intranet Access. *CAUSE/EFFECT, 20*(2):48-52. Available: http://cause-www.colorado.edu/. [7/27/01].

Green, K.C. (1996a). Campus Computing Survey. Pomona, CA: Claremont Graduate School.

Griffin, M.M., and Griffin, B.W. (1996). Situated cognition and cognitive style: Effects on students' learning as measured by conventional tests and performance assessments. *Journal of Experimental Education, 64*(4):293-308.

Hake, R.R. (1998). Interactive Engagement Versus Traditional Methods: A Six-Thousand Student Survey of Mechanics Test Data for Introductory Physics Courses. *American Journal of Physics, 66*:64-75.

Hall, R H. and Hickman, L.L. (1997, March). The Effect of Contiguity and Complexity of Web Page Displays on Subjective Ratings: The Role of Gender. Paper presented at the annual meeting of the American Educational Research Association, Chicago IL. Available: http://www.umr.edu/~rhall/research/aera/aera97.html. [7/27/01].

Halpern, D. (1992). *Sex differences in cognitive abilities.* 2nd Ed. Hillsdale, NJ: Erlbaum.

Hamilton, C.J. (1995). Beyond Sex Differences in Visuo-Spatial Processing: The Impact of Gender Trait Possession. *British Journal of Psychology, 86*:1-20.

Harley, S. (1993). Situated Learning and Classroom Instruction. *Educational Technology, 33*(3):46-51.

Helgeson, S.L. and Kumar, D.D. (1993). A Review of Educational Technology in Science Assessment. *Journal of Computers in Mathematics and Science Teaching, 12*(3/4):227-243.

Hellige, J. (1993). *Hemispheric asymmetry: What's right and what's left.* Cambridge, MA: Harvard University Press.

Herreid, C.F. (1997/1998). What Makes a Good Case? *Journal of College Science Teaching, 27*(3):163-165.

Herron, J.D. (1978). Piaget in the Classroom: Guidelines for Applications. *Journal of Chemistry Education, 55*(3):165-170.

Hilosky, A., Sutman, F., and Schmuckler, J. (1998). Is Laboratory-Based Instruction in Beginning College-Level Chemistry Worth the Effort and Expense? *Journal of Chemistry Education, 75*(1):100-104.

Holyoak, K.J. (1991). Symbolic Connectionism: Toward Third-Generation Theories of Expertise. Pp. 301-336 in K.A. Ericsson and J. Smith (Eds.), *Toward a general theory of expertise.* Cambridge, UK: Cambridge University Press.

Howard Hughes Medical Institute. (1996). *New tools for science education,* Undergraduate Program Directors' Meeting, October 25-27, 1995. Chevy Chase, MD: Author.

Howe, A.C. and Dowdy, W. (1989). Spatial Visualization and Sex-Related Differences in Science Achievement. *Science Education, 73*(6):703-709.

Hunt, W.T. (1992). Shared Understanding: Implications for Computer-Supported Cooperative Work. Qualifying exam paper, Department of Computer Science, University of Toronto. Available: http://www.dgp.utoronto.ca/people/WilliamHunt/qualifier.html. [7/27/01].

Iaccino, J.F. (1993). *Left brain-right brain differences: Inquiries, evidence, and new approaches.* Hillsdale, NJ: Lawrence Erlbaum.

International Technology Education Association. (2000). *Standards for technology education.* Reston, VA: Author. Available: http//www.itea.www.org. [7/27/01].

Johnson, D.W., Johnson, R.T., and Smith, K.A. (1998). Cooperative Learning Returns to College: What Evidence is there that it Works? *Change, 30*(4):27-35.

Johnson, J. (1997). It Takes a (Global) Village to Prepare Teachers: Teaching/Technology Reflection. *Selected Papers from the Eighth National Conference on College Teaching and Learning.* Jacksonville, FL: Florida Community College at Jacksonville.

Johnson, S.D. and Thomas, R.G. (1994). Implications of Cognitive Science for Instructional Design in Technology Education. *Journal of Technology Studies, 20*(1):33-45.

Jonassen, D.H., Campbell, J.P., and Davidson, M.E. (1994). Learning with Media: Restructuring the

Debate. *Educational Technology Research and Development*, 42(2):31-39.

Jones, B.F., Valdez, G., Nowakowski, J., and Rasmussen, C. (1996). *Plugging in: Choosing and using educational technology.* Oak Brook, IL: North Central Regional Educational Laboratory.

Jones, J.B. (1998). The Non-Use of Computers in Undergraduate Engineering Courses. *Journal of Engineering Education*, 87(1):11-14.

Jones, L.M. and Kane, D.J. (1994). Student Evaluation of Computer-Based Instruction in a Large University Mechanics Course. *American Journal of Physics*, 62(9):832-836.

Keefe, J. (1987). *Learning style: Theory and practice.* Reston, VA: National Association of Secondary School Principals.

Keller, J.M. (1987). Development and use of the ARCS model of motivational design. *Journal of Instructional Development*, 10(3):2-10.

Kershaw, A. (1996). People, Planning, and Process: The Acceptance of Technological Innovation in Post-Secondary Organizations. *Educational Technology*, XXXVI(5):44-48.

Khan, B.H. (Ed.) (1997). *Web-based instruction.* Englewood Cliffs, NJ: Educational Technology Publications Inc.

Kimura, D. (1987). Are Men and Women's Brains Really Different? *Canadian Psychology*, 28:133-147.

Kimura, D. (1992). Sex Differences in the Brain. *Scientific American*, 267(3):118-125.

King, J.E. (1998, May 1). Too Many Students Are Holding Jobs for Too Many Hours. *Chronicle of Higher Education*, p. A72.

Kolb, D. (1984). *Experiential learning: Experience as the source of learning and development.* Englewood Cliffs, NJ: Prentice Hall.

Kotovsky, K., Hayes, J.R., and Simon, H.A. (1985). Why Are Some Problems Hard? Evidence from the Tower of Hanoi. *Cognitive Psychology*, 17:248-294.

Kouzes, M., and Wulf, W.A. (2001). EMSL Collaborative. Available: http://www.emsl.pnl.gov:2080/docs/collab/CollabHome.html. [7/27/01].

Kozma, R.B., and Quellmalz, E.S. (1995). *Issues and needs in evaluating the educational impact of the national information infrastructure.* Menlo Park, CA: Center for Technology in Learning, SRI International. Paper presented at workshop sponsored by the Office of Educational Technology, U.S. Department of Education. Available: http://www.ed.gov/Technology/Futures/kozma.html [7/27/01].

Lanctot, R.C. (1998, March 11). U.S. Home PC Penetration Tops 45 Percent. *Computer Retail Week.* Available: http://www.techweb.com/wire/story/TWB19980311S0025 [7/27/01].

Larkin, J.H., McDermott, J., Simon, D., and Simon, H. (1980). Expert and Novice Performance in Solving Physics Problems. *Science*, 208:1335-1342.

Laurillard, D. (1993). *Rethinking university teaching: A framework for the effective use of technology.* London: Routledge.

Lave, J. and Wenger, E. (1991). *Situated learning: Legitimate peripheral participation.* Cambridge, UK: Cambridge University Press.

Laws, P.W. (1991). Calculus-Based Physics Without Lectures. *Physics Today*, Dec:24-31.

Laws, P.W. (1999). New Approaches to Science and Mathematics Teaching at Liberal Arts Colleges. *Daedalus*, 128(1):217-240.

Lehman, J.R. (1986). Microcomputer Offerings in Science Teacher Training. *School Science and Mathematics*, 86(2):119-125.

Levy, J. (1976). Cerebral Lateralization and Spatial Ability. *Behavior Genetics*, 6:171-188.

Linn, R.L., Baker, E.L., and Dunbar, S.B. (1991). Complex, Performance-Based Assessment: Expectation and Validation Criteria. *Educational Researcher*, 20:15-21.

Litzinger, M.E., and Osif, B. (1993). Accommodating diverse learning styles: Designing instruction for electronic information sources. In L.

Shirato, (Ed.) *What is good instruction now? Library instruction for the 90s.* Ann Arbor, MI: Pierian Press.

Macdonald, R.H. and Korinek, L. (1995). Cooperative Learning Activities in Large Entry-Level Geology Courses. *Journal of Geology Education, 43*:341-345.

MacLeod, C.M., Hunt, E.B., and Mathews, N.N. (1978). Individual Differences in the Verification of Sentence-Picture Relationships. *Journal of Verbal Learning and Verbal Behavior, 17*:493-508.

Massy, W.F., and Zemsky, R. (1996). Using Information Technology to Enhance Academic Productivity. *Educom Review, 31*(1):12-14. Available: http://www.educause.edu/nlii/keydocs/massy.html. [7/27/01].

Mayer, M. (1987). Common Sense Knowledge Versus Scientific Knowledge: The Case of Pressure, Weight and Gravity. Pp. 299-310 in *Proceedings of the second international seminar: Misconceptions and educational strategies in science and mathematics*, Vol. 1. Ithaca, NY: Cornell University Press.

Mazur, E. (1997). *Peer instruction.* Upper Saddle River, NJ: Prentice-Hall.

McCandless, G. (1998). Creating a Level Playing Field for Campus Computing: Universal Access. *Syllabus, 11*(6):12-14, 29. Available: http://www.syllabus.com [7/27/01].

McDermott, L.C. (1991). What we teach and what is learned-closing the gap. *American Journal of Physics, 59*:301-315.

McDermott, L.C., Shaffer, P., and Somers, M. (1994). Research as a guide for curriculum development: an illustration in the context of the Atwood's machine. *American Journal of Physics, 62*:46-55.

McLellan, H. (1993). Evaluation in a Situated Learning Environment. *Educational Technology, 33*(3):39-45.

McLellan, H. (1994). Situated Learning: Continuing the conversation. *Educational Technology, 34*(8):7-8.

McMillan, J.H., and Forsyth, D.R. (1991). What Theories of Motivation Say about How Learners Learn. Pp. 39-52 in R.J. Menges and M.D. Svinicki, (Eds.) *College teaching: From theory to practice.* New Directions in Teaching and Learning, No. 45. San Francisco: Jossey-Bass.

McNeal, A.P. and D'Avanzo, C. (Eds.) (1997). *Student-active science: Models of innovation in college science teaching.* Fort Worth, TX: Saunders College Publishing.

Means, B., and Olson, K. (1995). *Technology's role in education reform: Findings from a national study of innovating schools.* Washington, DC: U.S. Department of Education, Office of Educational Research and Improvement.

Millar, S.B., Kosciuk, S., Penberthy, D. and Wright, J.C. (1996). Faculty Assessment of a Freshman Chemistry Course. *Proceedings of the American Society for Engineering Education Annual Conference.* Washington, DC: American Society for Engineering Education, Session Number 2530.

Mislevy, R.J., and Gitomer, D. (1996). The Role of Probability-based Inference in an Intelligent Tutoring System. *User modeling and user-adapted interaction, 5*: 253-282.

Mitchell, W.J and Dertouzos, M.L, (Eds.) (1997). *MIT Educational Technology Council Report.* Cambridge, MA: MIT.

Morris, P.M., Ehrmann, S.C., Goldsmith, R.B., Howat, K.J., and Kumar, M.S.V. (Eds.) (1994). *Valuable, viable software in education: Case studies and analysis.* New York: PRIMIS-McGraw-Hill.

Mullis, I.V.S., Martin, M.O., Beaton, A.E., Gonzalez, E.J., Kelly, D.L., and Smith, T.A. (1998). *Mathematics achievement in the final year of secondary school: IEA's third international mathematics and science study.* Chestnut Hill, MA: Boston College, Center for the Study of Testing, Evaluation, and Educational Policy.

Munro, B.C. (1984). B. F. Skinner. *British Columbia Journal of Special Education,* 8(1):45-60.

Nakhleh, M.B. (1992). Why Some Students Don't Learn Chemistry. *Journal of Chemistry Education,* 69(3):191-196.

National Academy of Sciences. (1996). *Careers in science and engineering: A student planning guide to grad school and beyond.* Washington, DC: National Academy Press.

National Center for Education Statistics. (1998). *The condition of education, 1998.* Washington, DC: Author.

National Center for Improving Science Education. (1991). *The high stakes of high school science.* Washington, DC: Author

National Council for the Accreditation of Teacher Education. (1997). *Technology and the new professional teacher: Preparing for the 21st century classroom.* Washington, DC: Author. Available: http://www.ncate.org/pubs/m_pubs.htm#tech_prof_teach. [7/27/01].

National Council of Teachers of Mathematics. (1989). *Curriculum and evaluation standards for school mathematics.* Reston, VA: Author.

National Council of Teachers of Mathematics. (1991). *Professional standards for teaching mathematics.* Reston, VA: Author.

National Institute for Science Education. (1998). *Proceedings of the NISE forum on assessment.* Madison, WI: Author.

National Research Council. (1993). *National collaboratories: Applying information technology for scientific research.* Committee Toward a National Collaboration: Establishing the User Developer Partnership. Washington, DC: National Academy Press.

National Research Council. (1994a). *Information technology in the service society: A twenty-first century lever.* Committee to Study the Impact of Information Technology on the Performance of Service Activities. Washington, DC: National Academy Press.

National Research Council. (1994b). *Realizing the information future: The internet and beyond.* NRENAISSANCE Committee. Washington, DC: National Academy Press.

National Research Council. (1995). *Reshaping the graduate education of scientists and engineers.* Committee on Science, Engineering, and Public Policy. Washington, DC: National Academy Press.

National Research Council. (1996a). *From analysis to action: Undergraduate education in science, mathematics, engineering, and technology.* Center for Science, Mathematics, and Engineering Education. Washington, DC: National Academy Press.

National Research Council. (1996b). *National science education standards.* National Committee on Science Education Standards and Assessment. Washington, DC: National Academy Press.

National Research Council. (1996c). *The unpredictable certainty: Information infrastructure through 2000.* NII 2000 Steering Committee. Washington, DC: National Academy Press.

National Research Council. (1997a). *More than screen deep: Toward every-citizen interfaces for the nation's information infrastructure.* Toward an Every-Citizen Interface to the NII Steering Committee. Washington, DC: National Academy Press.

National Research Council. (1997b). *Adviser, teacher, role model, friend: On being a mentor to students in science and engineering.* Committee on Science, Engineering, and Public Policy. Washington, DC: National Academy Press.

National Research Council. (1998). *Developing a digital national library for undergraduate science, mathematics, engineering, and technology education.* Center for Science, Mathematics, and Engineering Education. Washington, DC: National Academy Press.

National Research Council. (1999a). *Being fluent with information technology.* Committee on

Information Technology Literacy. Washington, DC: National Academy Press.

National Research Council. (1999b). *How people learn: Brain, mind, experience and school.* Committee on Developments in the Science of Learning, J.D. Bransford, A.L. Brown, and R.R. Cocking (Eds.). Washington, DC: National Academy Press

National Research Council. (1999c). *Transforming education in science, mathematics, engineering, and technology.* Center for Science, Mathematics, and Engineering Education. Washington, DC: National Academy Press.

National Science Foundation. (1993). *Indicators of science and mathematics education.* Arlington, VA: Author.

National Science Foundation. (1996). *Shaping the future: New expectations for undergraduate education in science, mathematics, engineering, and technology.* Arlington, VA: Author.

National Science Foundation. (1998). *Information technology: Its impact on undergraduate education, science, mathematics, engineering and technology.* Available: http://www.nsf.gov/pubs/1998/nsf9882/nsf9882.pdf. [7/27/01].

National Science Teachers Association. (1998). *NSTA standards for science teacher education.* Arlington, VA: Author.

Naour, P. (1985). Brain/Behavior Relationships, Gender Differences, and the Learning Disabled. *Theory into Practice, 24(2):100-105.*

Neal, E. (1998, June 19). Using Technology in Teaching: We Need to Exercise Healthy Skepticism. *Chronicle of Higher Education,* p. B4.

Newell, A. and Simon, H.A. (1972). *Human problem solving.* Englewood Cliffs, NJ: Prentice Hall.

Niaz, M. (1991). *Reasoning strategies of students in solving chemistry problems as a function of developmental level, functional M-capacity and disembedding ability.* (ERIC Document Reproduction Service No. ED360180).

Norman, D.A. (1991). Cognitive Artifacts. Pp. 17-38 in John M. Carroll (Ed.), *Designing interac-*

tion: Psychology at the human-computer interface. Cambridge, UK: Cambridge University Press.

Norman, D.A. (1992). *Turn signals are the facial expressions of automobiles.* Reading, MA: Addison-Wesley.

Norman, D.A. (1993). *Things that make us smart.* Reading, MA: Addison-Wesley.

Novak, G.M., Patterson, E.T., and Gavrin, A.D. (1999). *Just-in time teaching: Blending active learning with Web technology.* Upper Saddle River, NJ: Prentice Hall.

Novak, G.M., Patterson, E.T., and Gavrin, A.D. (2001). A Brief Overview: What Is JiTT? Available: http://webphyics.iupui.edu/jitt/whatOVR.html. [9/25/01].

Novak, J.D. and Gowin, D.B. (1984). *Learning how to learn.* New York: Cambridge University Press.

Oberlin, J.L. (1996). The Financial Mythology of Information Technology: The New Economics. *Cause/Effect, Spring:* 21-29.

Okebukola, P.A. and Jegede, O. J. (1988). Cognitive preference and learning mode as determinants of meaningful learning through concept mapping. *Scientific Educator, 74:489-500.*

O'Loughlin, M. (1992). Rethinking Science Education: Beyond Piagetian Constructivism toward a Sociocultural Model of Teaching and Learning. *Journal of Research in Science Teaching, 29(8):791-820.*

Orlansky, J. and String, J. (1979). *Cost-effectiveness of computer-based instruction in military training.* Washington, DC: U.S. Department of Defense.

Osborne, J.F (1996). Beyond Constructivism. *Science Education, 80(1):53-82.*

Panitz, B. (1998). Learning on Demand. *American Society for Engineering Education Prism, 7(8):18-24.*

Pea, R. (1993). Practices of distributed intelligence and designs for education. Pp. 47-87 in G. Salomon (Ed.), *Distributed cognitions: Psychological and educational considerations.* Cambridge, UK: Cambridge University Press.

Pence, H.E. (1997). Are Simulations Just a Substitute for Reality? Paper #9, Summer On-Line Conference on Chemical Education, June 1-August 1.

Peters, P.C. (1982). Even Honors Students Have Conceptual Difficulties with Physics. *American Journal of Physics*, 50(6):501-508.

Pew Research Center for The People and The Press. (1995). Technology in the American Household. Available: http://www.people-press.org/tech.htm. [7/27/01].

Phillips, D.C. (1995). The Good, the Bad, and the Ugly: The Many Faces of Constructivism. *Educational Researcher*, 24(7):5-12.

Poole, B.J. and Kidder, S.Q. (1996). Making Connections in the Undergraduate Laboratory. *Journal of College Science Teaching*, 26(1):34-36.

Powers, P. (1998). One Path to Using Multimedia in Chemistry Courses: Enlivening Students' Learning Through Visual Presentations. *Journal of College Science Teaching*, 27:317-318.

President's Committee of Advisors on Science and Technology. Panel on Educational Technology. (1997). *Report to the President on the use of technology to strengthen K-12 education in the United States*. Washington, DC: U.S. Government Printing Office.

Project Kaleidoscope. (1991). *What works: Building natural science communities: A plan for strengthening undergraduate science and mathematics*. Volume I. Washington, DC: Author.

Project Kaleidoscope. (1994). *What works. Leadership: Challenges for the future*. Volume II. Washington, DC: Author.

Project Kaleidoscope. (1997). *The question of reform: Report on Project Kaleidoscope 1996-1997*. Washington, DC: Author.

Project Kaleidoscope. (1998). *Shaping the future of undergraduate science, mathematics, engineering and technology education: Proceedings and recommendations from the PKAL day of dialogue*. Washington, DC: Author.

Project Kaleidoscope. (1999). *Steps toward reform: Report on Project Kaleidoscope, 1997-1998*. Washington, DC: Author.

Rogoff, B. and Gardner, W. (1984). Adult Guidance of Cognitive Development. Pp. 95-116 in B. Rogoff and J. Lave (Eds.), *Everyday cognition*. Cambridge, MA: Harvard University Press.

Ruiz-Primo, M.A., Schultz, S.E., and Shavelson, R.J.. (1997). Concept Map-based Assessment in Science: Two Exploratory Studies. *CSE Technical Report 436*. Los Angeles: National Center for Research on Evaluation, Standards, and Student Testing.

Salomon, G. (1993). Editor's introduction. Pp. xi-xxi in G. Salomon (Ed.), *Distributed cognitions: Psychological and educational considerations*. Cambridge, UK: Cambridge University Press.

Schoenfeld, A.H. (1990). On mathematics as sense-making: An informal attack on the unfortunate divorce of formal and informal mathematics. In D.N. Perkins, J. Segal. and J. Voss (Eds.), *Informal reasoning and education*. Hillsdale, NJ: Erlbaum.

Schwartz, A.T., Bunce, D.M., Silberman, R.G., Stanitski, C.L., Stratton, W.J., and Zipp, A.P. (1997). *Chemistry in context*. 2nd ed. New York: McGraw-Hill.

Seymour, E. and Hewitt, N.M. (1997). *Talking about leaving: Why undergraduates leave the sciences*. Boulder, CO: Westview Press.

Seymour, E. and Hunter, A-B. (1998). *Talking about disability: The education and work experience of graduates and undergraduates with disabilities in science, mathematics, and engineering majors*. Washington, DC: American Association for the Advancement of Science.

Shaywitz, B.A., Shaywitz, S.E., Pugh, K.R., Constable, R.T., Skudlarskl, P., Fulbright, R.K., Bronen, R.A., Fletcher, J.M., Shankweller, D.P., Katz, L., and Gore, J.C. (1995). Sex Differences in the Functional Organization of the Brain for Language. *Nature*, 33:607-609.

Sherald, M., and Ward, S. (1994). Market Predictions with Backprop Neural Nets. *AI in Finance, Fall 1994*:25-30.

Shymansky, J.A., Yore, L.D., Treagust, D.F., Thiele, R.B., Harrison, A., Waldrip, B.G., Stocklmayer, S.M., and Venville, G. (1997). Examining the Construction Process: A Study of Changes in Level 10 Students' Understanding of Classical Mechanics. *Journal of Research in Science Teaching, 34*(6):571-593.

Simpson, R.D. and Frost, S.H. (1993). *Inside college: Undergraduate education for the future.* New York: Insight Books.

Sinnott, J. and Johnson, L. (1996). *Reinventing the university: A radical proposal for a problem-based university.* Norwood, NJ: Ablex Publishing Company.

Slavin, R.E. (1995). *Cooperative learning: Theory, research, and practice* (Second ed.). Boston: Allyn and Bacon.

Smith, S.G., Jones, L.L., and Waugh, M.L. (1986). Production and Evaluation of Interactive Videodisc Lessons in Laboratory Instruction. *Journal of Computer-Based Instruction, 13*:117-121.

Society for Industrial and Applied Mathematics. (1995). *The SIAM report on mathematics in industry.* Philadelphia, PA: Author. Available: http://www.siam.org/mii/miihome.htm. [7/27/01].

Software Publishers Association. (1997). *The effectiveness of technology in schools, '90-'97.* Washington, DC: Author.

Spitulnik, M.W and Krajcik, J. (1998). Technological Tools To Support Inquiry in a Science Methods Course. *Journal of Computers in Mathematics and Science Teaching, 17*(1):63-74.

Springer, L., Millar, S.B., Kosciuk, S. and Penberthy, D. (1997a). *Relating Concepts and Applications through Structured Active Learning.* Presented at the American Educational Research Association meeting, Chicago, IL.

Springer, L., Stanne, M.E., and Donovan, S. (1997b). *Effects of small-group learning on undergraduates in science, mathematics, engineering, and technology: A meta-analysis.* Madison, WI: National Institute for Science Education (pre-publication manuscript).

SRI Consulting. (1997). *Digital literacy: survival skills for the information age.* London, England: BIT3M Futurescript.

State of California. (1997). Interim County Population Projections. Sacramento, CA: Department of Finance. Available: http://www.dof.ca.gov/html/demograp/post2nd.htm. [7/27/01].

Sternberg, R.J. and Rifkin, B. (1979). The Development of Analogical Reasoning Processes. *Journal of Experimental Child Psychology, 27*:195-232.

Stevens, R.S., Lopo, A.C., and Wang, P. (1996). Artificial Neural Networks Can Distinguish Novice and Expert Strategies During Complex Problem Solving. *Journal of the American Medical Informatics Association, 3*:131-138.

Strassman, P. (1996, April 15). Spending without results? *Computerworld*, p. 88.

Sugrue, B. (1994). Specifications for the design of problem-solving assessments in science. *CSE Technical Report No. 387.* Los Angeles, CA: University of California, National Center for Research on Evaluation, Standards, and Student Testing.

Talley, L.H. (1973). The Use of Three-Dimensional Visualization as a Moderator in the Higher Cognitive Learning of Concepts in College Level Chemistry. *Journal of Research in Science Teaching, 10*:263-269.

Thomes, K. and Clay, K. (1998). University Libraries in Transition. *American Society of Engineering Education Prism, 7*(8):26-29.

Tinker, R. (1997). *The problem of extended inquiry in science teaching: Technology-rich curricula to the rescue.* Concord, MA: The Concord Consortium. Available: http://concord.org/pubs/extinq.html. [7/27/01].

Tissue, B.M. (1997). *The Costs of Incorporating Information Technology in Education.* Paper presented in the Summer On-Line Conference on Chemical Education, June 1-August 1.

Available: http://www.chem.vt.edu/archive/ chemconf97/paper04.html. [7/27/01].

Tobias, S. (1990). *They're not dumb, they're different: Stalking the second tier.* Tucson, AZ: Research Corporation.

Tobias, S. and Raphael, J. (1997a). *The hidden curriculum: Faculty-made tests in science. Part 1: Lower-division courses.* New York: Plenum.

Tobias, S. and Raphael, J. (1997b). *The hidden curriculum: Faculty-made tests in science. Part 2: Upper-division courses.* New York: Plenum.

Trefil, J. and Hazen, R.M. (1995). *The sciences: An integrated approach.* New York: Wiley.

Tripp, S.D. (1993). Theories, Traditions, and Situated learning. *Educational Technology, 33*(3):71-77.

Uecker, A. and Obrzut, J.E. (1993). Hemisphere and Gender Differences in Mental Rotation. *Brain and Cognition, 22*:42-50.

U.S. Department of Education. National Center for Education Statistics. (1996). *The condition of education 1996.* Washington, DC: U.S. Government Printing Office. Available: http:// nces.ed.gov/pubs/ce/c9609a01.html. [7/27/01].

Van Dusen, G.C. (1997). The Virtual University: Technology and Reform in Higher Education. *ASHE-ERIC Higher Education Report,* Volume 25, No. 5. Washington, DC: George Washington University.

von Glasersfeld, E. (1996). Footnotes to The Many Faces of Constructivism. *Educational Researcher, 25*(6):19.

Wang, R. (1996). *Learning chemistry in laboratory settings: A hands-on curriculum for non-science majors.* (ERIC Document Reproduction Service No ED399189.)

Watson, S.B. and Marshall, J.E. (1995). Effects of Cooperative Incentives and Heterogeneous Arrangement on Achievement and Interaction of Cooperative Learning Groups in a College Life Science Course. *Journal of Research in Science Teaching, 32*(3):291-299.

Weiner, B. (1990). History of Motivational Research in Education. *Journal of Educational Psychology, 82*:616-622.

Williamson, V.M. and Abraham, M.R. (1995). The Effect of Computer Animation on the Particulate Mental Models of College Chemistry Students. *Journal of Research in Science Teaching, 32*(5):521-534.

Wilson, A.L. (1993). The Promise of Situated Cognition. *New Directions for Adult and Continuing Education, 57*(3):71-80.

Wilson, B.J., Teslow, J., and Osman-Jouchoux, R. (1995). The Impact of Constructivism on Instructional Design Fundamentals. Pp. 137-157 in B.B. Seels (Ed.), *Instructional design fundamentals: A review and reconsideration.* Englewood Cliffs, NJ: Educational Technology Publications.

Wilson, J.M. (1994). The CUPLE Physics Studio. *The Physics Teacher, 32*:518.

Wilson, J.M. (1997). Distance Learning for Continuous Education. *EDUCOM Review, 32*(2):12-16. Available: http://educause.edu. [7/ 27/01].

Wittrock, M.C. (1974). Learning as a Generative Process. *Educational Psychologist, 11*:87-95.

Wright, J.C. (1996). Authentic Learning Environment in Analytical Chemistry Using Cooperative Methods and Open-Ended Laboratories in Large Lecture Courses. *Journal of Chemistry Education, 73*(9):827-832.

Wulf, W.A. (1989). The National Collaboratory: A White Paper. Appendix A in *Towards a National Collaboratory,* the unpublished report of an invitational workshop held at the Rockefeller University, March 17-18, 1989.

Young, J.R. (1998, March 13). For Students with Disabilities, the Web Can Be Like a Classroom without a Ramp. *The Chronicle of Higher Education,* p. A31.

Young, M.F. (1993). Instructional Design for Situated Learning. *Educational Technology, Research and Development, 41*(1):43-58.

Zoller, U. (1996). The Use of Examinations for Revealing and Distinguishing between Students' Misconceptions, Misunderstandings and "No Conceptions" in College Chemistry. *Research in Science Education, 26*(3):317-326.

Appendix B

Workshop Agenda

Workshop on the Roles of Information Technology in
Improving Teaching and Learning in Undergraduate
Science, Mathematics, Engineering and Technology Education
June 20-21, 2000

TUESDAY, JUNE 20, 2000

8:00 am   Continental Breakfast

8:15 am   **Welcome, Introductions, and Overview of Meeting**
         Mike Smith, Chair, Workshop Planning Group

9:00 am   **Session 1: Overview of Current Technologies in Teaching and Learning**
         Jean-Pierre Bayard, California State University, Sacramento

         Talk Title: *What's Out There: Instructional Technology for College-Level SME&T Instructors*

10:00 am   Break

10:15 am   Ron Stevens, UCLA

         Talk Title: *Tracing the Development, Transfer, and Retention of Problem-Solving Skills*

11:15 am   General Discussion

Noon   Lunch

| 1:00 pm | **Session 2: The Impact of Technology on Teaching and Learning** |
| | **a) What is the impact of current technology on teaching and learning?** |

Christopher Dede, George Mason University*

Talk Title: *Using Multiple Interactive Media to Enhance* Learning

Ben Shneiderman, University of Maryland

Talk Title: *Pedagogic Strategies for Applying Educational Technology: Relate-Create-Donate*

| 3:00 pm | Break |

| 3:15 pm | **b) Panel Discussion: How can the impact of technology on teaching and learning be evaluated most effectively?** |

Ron Stevens
Christopher Dede
Ben Shneiderman
Moderator: Mike Smith, Chair, Workshop Planning Group

| 5:15 pm | Summary of the day; plans for Day 2 |

WEDNESDAY, JUNE 21, 2000

| 8:00 am | Continental Breakfast |

| 8:15 am | **Session 3: Thinking about the Future of Information Technologies in Teaching and Learning** |

How to think about the future; looking at certainties and uncertainties, forces and drivers

Moderator: Alan Schwartz, PolicyFutures

---

*At the time of the workshop, Christopher Dede was at George Mason University. He is now at Harvard University.

9:00 am   **Four visions of transformative changes inside and outside the University**
Ted Kahn, President, DesignWorlds for Learning, Inc.; Principal, CapitalWorks, LLC

Chris Tucker, Chief Strategist, In-Q-Tel
Philip Agre, Department of Information Studies, University of California at Los Angeles

Richard Larson, Massachusetts Institute of Technology

10:00 am   Break

10:15 am   **Discussion of forces and drivers of change, and their implications**
Andries van Dam, Brown University

12:15 pm   **Lunch and Workshop Summary**

1:15 pm   Adjourn

Appendix C

Workshop Presenters and Participants

PRESENTERS

Day 1

Ronald Stevens, Director, IMMEX Software Development, University of California, Los Angeles

Jean-Pierre Bayard, Department of Electrical & Electronic Engineering, California State University, Sacramento

Christopher Dede, George Mason University*

Ben Shneiderman, University of Maryland

Day 2

Richard Larson, Massachusetts Institute of Technology

Ted Kahn, President, DesignWorlds for Learning, Inc.; Principal, CapitalWorks, LLC

Christopher Tucker, Chief Strategist, In-Q-Tel

PARTICIPANTS

Members of the Committee on Information Technology

Deborah Hughes Hallet, Professor of Mathematics, University of Arizona

Jack Wilson, Professor of Physics, Rensselaer Polytechnic Institute

---

*At the time of the workshop, Christopher Dede was at George Mason University. He is now a professor at Harvard University.

Stephen Hurst, University of Illinois
Dorothy Stout, National Science Foundation

Center for Education Strategic Planning Advisory Group

Mike Smith, Hewlett Foundation and Stanford University
Martha Darling, Educational Consultant
Melvin George, University of Missouri
Mike Atkin, Stanford University
Ron Latanision, Massachusetts Institute of Technology

NRC Staff

Kevin Aylesworth, Center for Education
Jay Labov, Center for Education
Michael Feuer, Center for Education
Ray Fornes, Government University Industry Research Roundtable
Terry Holmer, Center for Education

PolicyFutures

Alan Schwartz
Stanley Feder

Other Participants

Phil Agre, University of California, Los Angeles
Lara Couturier, Futures Project
Andries van Dam, Brown University
Diane Rogers, Chief of Staff to the Deputy Secretary of the U.S. Department of Education
Anne Morgan Spalter, Brown University
James Pellegrino, Vanderbilt University
Lee Zia, National Science Foundation

Appendix D

Planning Group Biosketches

Martha Darling is an education policy consultant in Ann Arbor, Michigan. Prior to moving to Ann Arbor, she worked in senior management at The Boeing Company in Seattle, Washington, from which she is now retired. At Boeing, she had assignments with the Commercial Airplane Group and also served as corporate manager of education affairs. In this capacity, she supported the CEO and other executives in their leadership roles in public education reform at the state level and in Seattle. Ms. Darling is active in a variety of civic and community organizations, serving on the boards of Reed College, the National Center for Research on Evaluation, Standards and Student Testing, the White House Fellows Foundation, and the Ann Arbor Hands-On Museum. Ms. Darling has also participated in a number of activities with the National Research Council (NRC) of the National Academies. She was vice chair of the National Advisory Committee for the former NRC Center for Science, Mathematics and Engineering Education and served as vice chair of the

advisory board of the NRC Center for Education.

Deborah Hughes Hallett is Professor of Mathematics at the University of Arizona. With Andrew M. Gleason at Harvard, she organized the Calculus Consortium based at Harvard, which brought together faculty from a wide variety of schools to improve undergraduate education in mathematics. With Gleason and other consortium members, Dr. Hughes Hallett has published several popular calculus textbooks that embody these improvements. Dr. Hughes Hallett is actively involved in discussions about the teaching of undergraduate mathematics at the national and international level. She is a member of the NRC's Committee on Advanced Study in American High Schools and of the Mathematical Association of America Committee on Mutual Concerns. She was chair of the American Women in Mathematics group that provided feedback to the National Council of Teachers of Mathematics when the council developed national mathematics education standards.

In 1998 she was co-chair of the International Conference on the Teaching of Mathematics in Samos, Greece, attended by faculty from 44 countries. Prior to this she established programs for mid-career master's students at the Kennedy School of Government, precalculus, and quantitative reasoning courses (with Gleason), and courses for economics majors. She was awarded the Louise Hay Prize and elected a fellow of the American Association for the Advancement of Science for contributions to mathematics education.

Marshall S. Smith is education program officer with the William and Flora Hewlett Foundation, on leave from the School of Education at Stanford University. Dr. Smith is the former undersecretary and acting deputy secretary of the U.S. Department of Education. He trained originally in statistical techniques for research, and acquired extensive knowledge of policy issues through his years of academic experience. He has held key positions in government education policy during the 1970's; researched topics including computer analysis of social science data, early child education, critical thinking, and social inequality; and taught at Harvard, Wisconsin, and Stanford. At Stanford, he was dean of the School of Education for six years. With this broad background, he is able to integrate research on policy questions from several disciplines and to focus on educational process, whether at the level of the individual student in the classroom or at the level of state and national educational reform. Dr. Smith is a member of the National Academy of

Education, Co-Chair of the Pew Forum on Education Reform, and Principal Investigator of the Pew Network on District Reform. He participated in the NRC Committee on Information Technology and on the Center for Education's Strategic Planning Advisory Group. Dr. Smith received his EdD degree in Measurement and Statistics at Harvard University in 1970.

Jack Wilson is professor of management at the University of Massachusetts, Amherst, and CEO of UMassOnLine, which offers University of Massachusetts courses on the Internet. Formerly, Wilson was J. Eric Jonsson Distinguished Professor of Physics, Engineering Science, Information Technology, and Management at Rensselaer Polytechnic Institute, and co-director of RPI's Severino Center for Technological Entrepreneurship. He founded and was chairman of the board of Interactive Learning International (ILINC), and later became chief scientist of Mertergy Corporation. He joined the faculty of Rensselaer in 1990 and moved to the University of Massachusetts in 2001. Among the many awards he has won, Dr. Wilson received the Pew Charitable Trusts Leadership Award for Renewal of Undergraduate Education in 1996. Dr. Wilson has published numerous papers, one of which is "Re-engineering the Undergraduate Curriculum," a book chapter for *The Learning Revolution* published by Anker Publishing Co. in 1997. Dr. Wilson received his A.B. from Thiel College in 1967, and his M.A. and Ph.D. from Kent State University in 1972.